REDEFINING
GIRLY

REDEFINING GIRLY

How Parents Can Fight the
STEREOTYPING and SEXUALIZING
of Girlhood, from Birth to Tween

MELISSA ATKINS WARDY

foreword by
JENNIFER SIEBEL NEWSOM

First edition
Published by Chicago Review Press, Incorporated
814 North Franklin Street
Chicago, Illinois 60610
ISBN 978-1-61374-552-6

Interior design: PerfecType, Nashville, TN
Cover design: Natalya Balnova
Cover photo: Emely/Cultura/Getty Images

Library of Congress Cataloging-in-Publication Data
Wardy, Melissa Atkins.
    Redefining girly : how parents can fight the stereotyping and sexualizing of girl-
hood, from birth to tween / Melissa Atkins Wardy ; foreword by Jennifer Siebel
Newsom.
        pages cm
    Summary: "Containing practical, specific parenting advice; strategies for effecting
change with educators, store managers, corporations, and more; and tips for challenging and changing the media, this essential guide gives parents the tools they
need to fight back against the modern stereotyping and sexualization of young girls.
Activist Melissa Wardy shares tangible advice for getting young girls to start thinking critically about sexed-up toys and clothes while also talking to girls about body
image issues. She provides tips for creating a home full of diverse, inspiring toys
and media free of gender stereotypes, using consumer power to fight companies that
make such major missteps, and taking the reins to limit, challenge, and change the
harmful media and products bombarding girls. Redefining Girly provides specific
parenting strategies, templates, and sample conversations and includes letters from
some of the leading experts in education, psychology, child development, and girls'
advocacy"— Provided by publisher.
    Summary: "This essential guide gives parents the tools they need to fight back
against the modern stereotyping and sexualization of young girls"— Provided by
publisher.
    Includes bibliographical references and index.
    ISBN 978-1-61374-552-6 (pbk.)
    1. Girls. 2. Girls—Psychology. 3. Stereotypes (Social psychology) 4. Sex role in
children. 5. Child rearing. I. Title.

HQ777.W374 2014
305.23082—dc23

                                    2013029063
Printed in the United States of America
5 4 3 2 1

This book is dedicated to the girls, big and small,
who are waiting for the world to see just how smart, daring,
and adventurous they are.

Closest to my heart—this book is for Amelia and Benny,
my little loves and endless mischief makers.
And to Clara Grace, Madeline, and Alexander:
wherever you are in the world, I love you.

"The most difficult thing is the decision to act,
the rest is merely tenacity."

—Amelia Earhart

Contents

Foreword by Jennifer Seibel Newsom   xi

Prologue: The Birth of an Activist   3

1 What Does It Mean to Redefine Girly?   13

2 Redefining Girly Starts Before Birth   17

3 How to Start Redefining Girly in Your Home   25

4 Getting Family and Friends on Board   35

5 Encouraging Kids at Play—The Diverse Toy Box   59

6 Around the Kitchen Table—Fat Talk and Body Image   89

7 Navigating Too Sexy Too Soon Birthday Parties
   and Holidays   113

8 Getting Your Kids' Educators and Health Care Providers
   on Your Side   135

9 Shopping Strategies—Saying No to Sexed-Up Clothes
   and Yes to a Personal Brand   161

10 Using Your Voice and Consumer Power to Fight
   the Companies Making Major Missteps   173

11 Becoming the Media You Want to See   195

Acknowledgments   213

Resources   217

Bibliography   227

Index   231

Foreword

This book, *Redefining Girly* by Melissa Atkins Wardy, is a godsend to parents. As the mother of a young girl, a young boy, and a newborn girl, I am, like Melissa, frustrated, agitated, and overwhelmed by the power marketers hold over our culture and the way in which they bombard us with limiting and very dangerous notions of what it means to be a girl and what it means to be a boy today.

Melissa's reasoning for writing this guide mirrors many of the reasons I made the film *Miss Representation* and remain committed to creating films and social-action campaigns that shift individual and community consciousness, and in turn prompt action.

Melissa and I both agree that today's media are sending a very dangerous message that women's and girls' value and power lie in their sexuality and not in their capacity as leaders. This only reinforces and adds to the unconscious sexism and bias toward women in our culture that prevents women from realizing their full human potential.

When I first realized I was pregnant with a girl, I was terrified by the thought of raising a daughter in a culture that so regularly demeans, degrades, and disrespects women and girls. As I set out to make *Miss Representation*, it became increasingly clear how pervasive both the objectification and self-objectification of women had become in our society. From the hypersexualized images girls see in advertising to the limited spectrum of professional women seen on-screen in television and film, mainstream media provide very little inspiration for our daughters. Marketers have so bifurcated gender in order to push more products to America's families that they are selling our kids a bill of limited goods. Our young girls, right out of the womb, are sold the notion that their value lies in their youth, their beauty, and their sexuality, while their brothers and male peers are taught early on that boys are our natural-born leaders and that domination, control, and aggression can be utilized to preserve the status quo.

The situation is dire! The media is pressuring our girls at younger and younger ages to conform to a warped and hypersexualized version of girlhood and womanhood. As a consequence, we see unprecedented rates of low self-esteem issues and serious health problems such as eating disorders, anxiety, depression, drug and alcohol abuse, cutting, bullying, and suicide attempts, further prohibiting girls from becoming leaders.

It's rather hypocritical, isn't it, that we tell our daughters and future generations that they can be whatever they want to be when they grow up, when in fact the media and therefore our greater culture limits women in so many ways? Given these barriers to entry, it's no wonder that we culturally accept that a man in leadership is more valuable than a woman. This can be noted generally, with women's leadership peaking at 18 percent representation in business, politics, military, religion, media, culture, and entertainment—something that is easily forgotten when one woman makes it to the top. So women might be 51 percent of the population, and give birth to 100 percent of the population, but they remain underrepresented in leadership across the board.

Miss Representation and MissRepresentation.org are my attempts to right this wrong and put our culture on a path that recognizes, empowers, and inspires women and girls to realize their dreams. Women and girls must no longer be portrayed as second-class citizens but rather as equals to men and boys, with the same opportunities to succeed in life.

But we cannot do this work alone! We need parents, families, and communities to stand up and take notice of the major public-health crisis on our hands. It starts with shifting family consumer habits. For example, let's choose dolls for our girls that have realistic body shapes and healthy aspirations, such as Go! Go! Sports Girls; let's encourage them to play with stuffed animals, which are great tools for modeling relationships and practicing nurturing, something that all kids like to role-play; and finally, how about giving a second thought to the corporate marketing–driven princess culture?! Why do all our little girls dream of being princesses? Because Disney tells them to! As my friend Geena Davis says, "Being a princess is a nice job if you can get it!" But think about it: the word *princess* reeks of privilege, entitlement, and someone out of touch with the real world. A princess's sole purpose in life is to be pretty enough to attract the attention of a male suitor—a knight in shining armor on a white horse—who will rescue her and take care of her. She is never required to hold a job. Sure, childhood is a time for make-believe, but do these retrograde messages make sense in an era when well over half of all adult women work outside the home?

It is clear to me that the vast majority of marketers and content creators have no interest in the mental health of our children—it's all about the bottom line and their own paychecks. So we must take matters into our own hands by stopping the chain of consumption.

I commend Melissa for her courage and conviction in writing this exceptional guide. It's so easy to feel alone and overwhelmed as a parent in this fight against the worst of corporate America and our media culture, which wants to sell sex and violence 24/7 to our kids in order to continue to churn profits. I hope that every parent, grandparent, aunt, and uncle across the country, not to mention every child care provider, school educator, administrator, health care professional, coach, youth group leader, and afterschool supervisor will use *Redefining Girly* as their go-to resource for raising healthy and happy children.

In the meantime, Melissa, you, and all of us in partnership with MissRepresentation.org will keep working to overcome the media and our greater culture's limiting notions about what it means to be a girl and what it means to be a boy. We will be vigilant and mandate that those in positions of authority around our kids don't fall prey to gender stereotypes but instead help our kids realize their human potential. This means stopping the reinforcement of gender stereotypes in the classroom, on the playground, in the waiting room, and at home.

Moms, let's not forget we are so much more than our youth, our beauty, and our sexuality. Let's take our daughters on adventures, teach them about finance, and not be afraid to get down and dirty with them on the soccer field in the rain. And if you take them on a "girls' outing" to get a mani-pedi, be sure to communicate that it's more about self-care than vanity and self-objectification. I am a huge proponent of women learning self-care (especially when we moms have such little time to take care of ourselves).

And dads, you can help by paying attention to how you speak about and value women in your daughters' presence. Don't forget to help out with the cooking, the cleaning, and the caregiving—you'll be modeling a healthier image of what it means to be a man so that your daughters (and sons) can aspire to an equal partnership someday.

Who knows what will become of your daughter? Raise her to fulfill her potential and she just might be a great mom *and* the president of the United States!

Jennifer Siebel Newsom is the writer, director, and producer of *Miss Representation* and the founder and CEO of MissRepresentation.org.

REDEFINING
GIRLY

Prologue

The Birth of an Activist

When my husband and I decided we were ready to start our family, I felt like I would have this parenting thing in the bag. I had babysat frequently in high school, worked as a camp counselor, and been a nanny for years in college. I figured there wasn't anything kids could throw my way that I had not already seen. As it turned out, kids were the easy part. It took me about six months as a parent to realize that it was the media and the marketplace that were going to provide the biggest bumps in the road for our family.

Amelia came into our world on a snowy morning and I was awestruck. She was so tiny and breathtaking with her soft pink skin and raven black hair. We didn't know her sex before she was born, so most of her clothes were white or pale yellow. A layette of white seemed to me to represent the blank canvas of a newborn's life. After bringing her home from the hospital we started to receive gifts to celebrate her birth: a gown with tiny rosebud flowers and the red ladybug outfit were darling, and I squealed when I opened them. I was delighted at the sweetness of my new girl and the beautiful things filling her world. A pink stuffed bunny here and a blanket with softly colored kittens there seemed really cute. I paid little attention to the colors or messages of her new clothes and toys, and didn't really see any reason to. I was a happy, confident mother enjoying my baby girl.

My daughter was six months old when I suddenly came to feel uneasy. I was shopping at Target after Amelia's six-month checkup, buying the infant toothbrush her pediatrician had recommended for the four teeth she had popped. I stood in the aisle looking at my choices: Disney princesses, Dora the Explorer, or SpongeBob SquarePants. I grabbed Dora, although at the time I didn't really know who Dora was. I just thought she was cute, with her dark hair and round tummy, and looked like what my girl would look like in a few years.

Next I headed over to the baby section for a big moment: the selection of our first sippy cup. I pulled the cart up to the wall and was faced with cups adorned with the likes of *Toy Story* characters or, again, princesses. No princes, mind you, just pink and purple Disney princesses, postured daintily in their princess poses. I think there was Mickey Mouse or Diego, too, which I guessed were meant for the boys. For the girls, though, it seemed princesses were the primary offering. I finally found a plain yellow and blue cup without any characters on it, threw it into the cart, and then headed to the toy section to look for some stacking toys, balls, and peg puzzles because Amelia was just beginning to crawl and because I thought she was a baby genius.

As I walked through the toy aisles, these are the themes I noticed, and I do not exaggerate:

Girls = baby dolls, baby care items, princesses (all Disney), sexy fashion dolls whose faces and bodies look like they have been surgically altered, beauty/makeup toys, play cooking and baking sets, animal care toys, and crafts.

Boys = monsters, action or war figures, superheroes, rescue or action vehicles, building blocks and kits, sports and outdoor toys, guns and weapons, scientific experiment kits, and dinosaurs.

That was it. There was no middle ground. I didn't see any dolls or cooking sets for boys, nor building blocks or fire trucks for girls. There was nothing in the way of gender neutrality. If a boy was interested in cooking, he would have had to go into the "girl aisle" and choose something dipped in pink. If a girl wanted an action figure or a Lego set, she very clearly had to walk into the "boy aisle" to get it.

There was nothing that showed boys and girls playing together. Even the board games had become gendered. How can memory games and checkers have a boy version and a girl version? There was very little that resembled the childhood I remembered. I had trouble understanding why the toys for girls were so focused on domesticity or looking sexy. I did not remember Barbie dressing so provocatively, and what in the world was a Bratz doll?

What strange land was I in? This was the new childhood? This was how I was supposed to raise my girl? I didn't yet have the words to describe what I was looking at, but I knew it wasn't healthy for little girls. I knew it in my heart and felt it in my gut.

A couple months later, we moved from the Washington, DC area where we were living and purchased our first home in southern Wisconsin. My husband and I wanted to be closer to family, and the ideal Midwest childhood seemed very appealing to us. We chose a tidy two-story Cape Cod within a block of what would become our elementary school. There were two city playgrounds and a giant grassy field within walking distance. Shady trees and wide sidewalks made this little house perfect for our family. I had visions of kite flying and T-ball and soccer games and playing fetch with the dogs.

I was so excited to set up Amelia's nursery in the new house. I picked out a cheery bumblebee yellow for her walls, hung sage green curtains, added a wallpaper border with bright colors and cute garden bugs, and framed some photographs of white flowers that I had found at the farmer's market. The decor felt complete—until I noticed I had neglected to buy a cute light switch plate. I made a mental note to add it to the list for the next time we were at the hardware store.

It was a few months after my disturbing sippy cup shopping trip, when my husband and I were out hunting for that perfect light switch plate for Amelia's sunny new garden bug–themed room, that I first verbalized my growing frustration. A smiling ladybug or friendly grasshopper wouldn't be too hard to find, right? Wrong. Our conversation that day went something like this:

"This just drives me nuts!" I say to my husband while he is making faces at Amelia as she sits in the shopping cart.

"What drives you nuts? Just pick one," my husband says of the array of plates, not seeing the forest through the trees. Actually, the poor guy has no idea he is about to enter the woods.

"This. Every choice for girls is covered in princesses and tiaras. Look at all the boy choices, look at all of the colors," I say as I feel my blood pressure rise.

"So pick a boy one. Get one with footballs!" my husband suggests.

"There should be more choices for girls." I am becoming exasperated. I'm also wondering why there even *are* boy versions and girl versions of light switch plates.

"So get a plain one and just decorate it yourself," my husband offers as I glare at him.

"You are so missing the point here. It is about choices and marketing and gender identity. It is the principle of it, honey."

"Are we still talking about light switch plates? Because I have no idea what you are talking about. Do you know what she is talking about?" my husband asks baby Amelia as she blows spit bubbles and kicks her legs wildly.

And he didn't have any idea what I was talking about. I felt like I had been learning a new language recently, having just read *Packaging Girlhood: Rescuing Our Daughters from Marketers' Schemes* by Lyn Mikel Brown and Sharon Lamb, and was experiencing a fundamental shift in how I saw myself as a parent to a little girl. I was learning a whole new vocabulary that described the things I was seeing firsthand—concepts such as early sexualization and binary gender marketing, age compression and princess culture, "pinkification," and body image obsession. I was coming to understand how the limited colors and hypergendered messages of the clothes and toys and products being marketed to girls, even as babies (an infant purse with a diamond ring, lipstick, and credit card, anyone?), limited Amelia and also limited how people viewed her.

I had quickly come to realize that raising my daughter would involve more than just day-to-day stuff like feeding her healthy foods and having a smooth bedtime routine and baby proofing the house and teaching her to talk. I needed to worry about more than the big stuff, like instilling good manners and kindness and a love of learning. I realized that my husband and I needed to be gatekeepers with the media and products that were entering our home. No small task.

My eyes had been opened. The marketing of sexualized toys and clothing, distorted body types in both boys' and girls' dolls, gender distortion in children's media, and age compression—adult products and attitudes being pushed on younger and younger kids—were corrupting our young sons' and daughters' right to a carefree childhood. Once you see it, you can't unsee it, and I was seeing it everywhere.

This was a perversion of childhood that disrespected the wonderful, creative, whimsical people our children are. This was not good enough for my children. I would not accept it. I decided to devote my time to researching the problems and creating change.

I started reading. I reached out and talked to people, took a gamble and e-mailed a few of the experts from the websites listed in their books or blogs. They replied, and I listened. I kept reading and reading and talking and talking. I became convinced that we as a society aren't having a conversation that needs to be had. Or, better put, parents aren't provided with the information early enough in our parenting experiences to have these conversations and come up with action items. I know moms and dads all over who *are* talking about the sexualization of childhood but feel isolated and powerless to do anything about it. Parents are not finding enough ways to aggregate our voices, and we are unsure of how to combat this media and marketing juggernaut we know to be unhealthy for our kids. We have to figure all of this sexualization garbage out on our own, and then we feel like we're standing on an island once our eyes have been opened. Why isn't this kind of thinking mainstream? Why don't my pediatrician or the parenting magazines talk about sexualization and teaching healthy body image? Why are companies given free rein to sell toys and clothing with messages that the American Psychological Association (APA) has confirmed hurt our kids?

In 2007 the APA released the findings from its Task Force on the Sexualization of Girls. The group made an important distinction between sexualization and sexuality, noting, "when children are imbued with adult sexuality, it is often imposed upon them rather than chosen by them. Self-motivated sexual exploration, on the other hand, is not sexualization by our definition, nor is age-appropriate exposure to information about sexuality."

It went on to say that "ample evidence . . . indicates that sexualization has negative effects in a variety of domains, including cognitive functioning, physical and mental health, sexuality, and attitudes and beliefs." Although most of the studies involved older teens, the task force suggested what concerned parents of young girls instinctively know to be true, that "findings are likely to generalize to younger adolescents and to girls, who may be even more strongly affected because their sense of self is still being formed."

The study found that sexualization is present not only in every form of our omnipresent media (television, movies, music, lyrics, video games, magazines, advertising, sports) but is also enacted by parents placing emphasis on girls maintaining an attractive physical appearance, by adults encouraging girls to "play" at being sexualized older women or suggesting they are incapable of high academic achievement, by kids' peers policing one another over the ideal of thinness and sexiness or sexually harassing and objectifying one another. At the extreme end are sexual abuse, sexual assault, prostitution, and sex trafficking.

What does it look like when girls internalize sexualization? The APA found they will purchase (or ask their parents to purchase) products and apparel designed to make them look more physically appealing and sexy. Oftentimes these styles mirror those of sexy celebrities. Girls also sexualize themselves when they think about and treat their bodies as the object of someone else's desires. "In self-objectification," the findings read, "girls internalize an observer's perspective on their physical selves and learn to treat themselves as objects to be looked at and evaluated for their appearance." In other words, no, all little girls are not "naturally" into fashion and makeup and "girly" trappings as some would suggest; rather, we as a society are pushing them hard in that direction at increasingly younger ages.

Knowing all this, now that my daughter is eight, I feel angry. Like, someone-came-up-and-kicked-Mama Bear-in-the-face angry. I believe the sexualization of childhood will soon be seen as the children's rights issue of our time. Sexualization affects both boys and girls of all ages but is especially focused on our girls. Sexualization affects all races, economic classes, and geographic areas. It robs children of their right to childhood and to reach psychological developmental milestones fairly, and it affects their self-esteem, body image, and performance in school. Sexualization interferes with kids' right to develop a healthy sexuality and understanding of intimacy. It can rush them into sexual experimentation and cause problems in future intimate relationships. It causes girls to seek validation from external sources, largely based on their sex appeal and measuring up to a narrowly defined version of beauty known as "the beauty myth."

The problem of sexualization goes hand in hand with the earliest stereotypes of what it means to be a boy (rough, rowdy, and into action) and what it means to be a girl (sweet, docile, and into "frivolous" pursuits). How quickly the marketing machines go from pushing "sweet and pretty" little girls' products to "sassy and sexy" tween and young adult merchandise.

We as parents need to stop this snowball before it starts rolling. Childhood does not naturally have a boy side and a girl side, certainly not in the first several years. I see childhood as a time for brightly colored, unstructured play fueled by powerful imaginations and driven by the understanding all young children seem to have that the world is their oyster. While certain children may gravitate to specific interests and types of play, after working with children for more than twenty years and raising a son and a daughter, I remain unconvinced these interests are driven by their biological sex. There is so much for our children to learn, why limit them with gender stereotypes?

The commercial sexualization of childhood has gotten to the point where parents often have to go out of their way and sometimes spend twice the amount of money in order to keep their home free of clothing, toys, and media that sexualize and stereotype their children. Yet there *are* easy ways to keep your home media literate and gender equal—full of playthings that allow for open-ended play and lots of imagination. I certainly will not be teaching my daughter, named after the great adventurer Amelia Earhart, to sit quietly and be pretty. I flatly refuse to teach her that her beauty is her only source of worth. I raise my girl to be smart, daring, and adventurous. I don't think those things belong on the "boy side" of the aisle; they belong right in the middle of childhood. By the same token, I raise my son to be intelligent, caring, and kind. He loves his pink toothpaste, superheroes, playing with our toy kitchen, and playing daddy to a stuffed puppy. I just allow him to be a little boy, and he gets to decide what that means.

When I was brand-new to parenting, I didn't have the words to express what I was feeling and noticing. I knew this wasn't right for my girl, but when I would talk to my friends about it they would shrug or make fun of me. I was told to lighten up, get over myself, or to stop being such a "feminazi." Maybe you've heard some version of these things too.

Still, I held on. I knew girls deserved better. Girls deserved more. My little girl deserved more. Your girl deserves more.

In the past several years I have seen parents awaken to the problems of gender stereotypes and sexualization of increasingly younger children. Many helpful books and articles have been written on these issues by many brilliant and highly credentialed authors from whom I have learned a great deal. These writers and activists continue to inspire me, and many of them have generously contributed heartfelt letters written directly to you—concerned parents—which appear in these pages. But what I felt was missing from the dialogue, what I felt other parents were missing, was a tool kit of really practical, parent-tested, and proven strategies and ideas from a mom in the trenches, help for parents to navigate through all this with their families and also practical things you can do *right now* to effect real change in the culture at large.

I want to help other parents benefit from what my family has tried and what has worked: creating homes and play spaces where childhood thrives in a creative, organic way; having talking points ready when discussing these issues with friends and family; being armed with information and responses when talking to your child's teachers and principals, doctors and dentists; teaching critical thinking skills to our children; and finally, encouraging—sometimes demanding—marketers and media to do better by our girls. While my parenting experiences are limited to the days spent with my eight-year-old daughter and five-year-old son, I have spent the past four years speaking with thousands of parents of girls. For this book I interviewed a couple dozen parents of tween girls to see what lies ahead for Amelia and me.

A few years ago, feeling pressure and sadness from the realizations I had made about the state of girlhood, I felt lost at sea. I felt as if there needed to be a monumental shift in the way our society thought about our girls.

Now I know this to be true. Now I know my way. Let's join together to make a better childhood for our girls.

What Does It Mean to Redefine Girly?

As my eyes opened to the entwined problems of stereotyping and sexualization of ever-younger girls, a gnawing question wouldn't quiet down in my brain: Why in the world is my generation—including the most educated, well-traveled, worldly, and accomplished generation of women ever—allowing our girls to be raised in a cultural context of sleeping princesses and sassy, looks-obsessed pop stars? Surely we could do better and demand more.

During a playdate in 2006, when Amelia was a baby, a friend was challenging my stance on Disney princesses and why I didn't like them, when I retorted with something about not being crazy about the idea of teaching my daughter to wish on a star and wait for a prince, but rather wanting her to have the know-how to build a rocket ship and get to that star for herself. I said something about being sick of pink tiaras and wanting to give Amelia a different vision of being a girl but was unable to find anything as simple as a pilot or an astronaut on a T-shirt for a little girl. Hello, a-ha moment! I scooped up baby Amelia, ran out of the house, and raced home to fill two notebooks with ideas for an apparel and toy company that would offset the void I saw.

Later that night, as I was talking with my husband about all these ideas, I tried to convey that there needed to be a broader definition of girlhood. I tried explaining why I thought that tea parties, fancy hair ribbons, tutus, fairy wings, and princess stories were all a fun part of childhood, but with Disney having such a huge hold over the market-place, princesses came in only one dainty variety and fairies came in tiny green dresses in poses reminiscent of the woman on the back of a semitruck's mud flap. I couldn't understand why there were no pirate or Lara Croft dolls or building and construction stuff in the girl aisles. Where were the detective kits and space or wildlife exploration toys? The message a consumer got in the mainstream toy aisles was that the most adventurous thing a girl might be interested in was becoming a veterinarian.

My husband agreed with much of what I was saying. He said he pictured taking our little girl to ballet class just as easily as tossing a football with her, teaching her to throw a spiral. Much like me, he had no use for passive princesses and all-pink products. He was very turned off by the sexy dolls and the "sassy" theme in girls' clothing. Already the protective father, he was uneasy about the sexualization of little girls and what it meant for their health and safety.

It felt really good to talk to him about these things and to know that he supported how I felt about the childhood I wanted Amelia to have. Yes, I was excited for her to grow bigger so that we could enjoy an outdoor tea party with lemonade and fancy cookies. I just expected we'd be doing that in celebration of capturing a crew of imaginary pirates and tying them to the tree fort as we walked away with their treasure. I wanted her childhood to be balanced. As we talked it became clear to me: We had to change our definition of what it meant to be "girly." We had to include all the amazing things girls were inter-ested in and good at. We had to redefine girly.

The company I would come to form around this idea of redefining girly launched in May 2009 and has given me the opportunity to speak with tens of thousands of parents. Now four years in business, Pigtail

Pals & Ballcap Buddies has shipped empowering products to all fifty states and to fifteen countries. My social media sites and blog are active and incredible places for discussion as parents unpack and digest what is going on around their girls. There is most definitely a space in the marketplace for products and companies that empower, inspire, and build up our girls. In fact, things were going so well that in May 2012 I expanded the company to include and advocate for boys.

> Tip: Make a list with your partner of the top ten memories you each hold from childhood. Make a point to give your daughter all those same experiences. ❋

Redefining girly means that our girls will show the world they are more than demure princesses, sassy divas, or spoiled brats. It means our girls cannot be packaged and boxed into a stereotype. It means not all girls are the same. Our girls will show the world the great potential, intellect, and talents they hold. It means our girls are not defined by their gender. Redefining girly means we can expect the same great things for our daughters, and from our daughters, as we do our sons.

Redefining girly means a girl can love riding horses or building robots or painting or ballet or catching bugs or smashing a softball, and all of those things are girly. Redefining girly means doing away with the labels "girly girl" and "tomboy." The stereotypical girly girl pursuits are often unfairly viewed as frivolous by society, and the idea that a girl loving sports or science or nature is being "boyish" is sexist and insulting. Most girls are not so two-dimensional. Most girls I know are the best of both worlds. My own girl loves dressing up and art. She's never met a mud puddle or a bug she didn't like. She rarely plays with baby dolls, opting instead for "ocean animal rescue center." She is what society calls a girly girl *and* a tomboy, usually both in the same day.

Just as girls come in all shapes and sizes, so too do their personalities. Some girls truly do love princesses and fashion and baby dolls. Other girls only have eyes for science and sports. The important thing is to provide a childhood and a home where your daughter is exposed to everything, and let her choose her path. We need fashion designers and devoted stay-at-home moms just as much as we do electrical engineers and champion athletes. Our girls need the space to try it all, and follow where their hearts lead them.

We need to accept all girls as they are and encourage all of their interests, from taking care of babies to learning how to use tools, from shooting hoops to wearing a tiara. What I wish the families raising daughters to know is that there is no single right way to be a girl. The possibility that grows inside your girl each day is limitless.

Redefining girly means we will not limit our girls to the ideas and toys marketed to them, but rather let our girls define for themselves who they will be in this world.

Redefining Girly Starts Before Birth

Most people make the jump into parenting with little understanding of children's media and marketing. How could they? Media literacy—the ability to analyze, evaluate, and create messages in a wide variety of media modes, genres, and forms—is not a skill our culture talks much about or assigns value to, and it's the rare young couple without kids who are actively tuned in to products and media marketed to children.

I can see how new parents get swept away in gendered marketing without even realizing it is there. There is such excitement and newness to having a baby and registering for gifts. All the new items coming into your home for your baby look adorable. Most couples are not thinking about gender stereotypes when they are picking out nursery decor, they are simply joyful over the idea of creating a happy home for their growing family.

If these couples were to take a step back and take in the big picture of children's marketing, they would notice these prevailing themes as they shopped for infant nursery bedding and room decorations:

Girls: flowers, butterflies, pink animals, ballerinas, princesses, and feminine patterns

Boys: cars, trucks, planes, trains, ships, animals in their normal colors, Noah's Ark, Wild West, pirates, and sports

And so it begins, before your baby is even born; the messages marketed to soon-to-be new baby boys and girls are very different. Girls will be told with no words at all to be pretty and delicate and stay close to home, while boys are urged to be masters of their universe and travel around their great big world. The girls' colors are very soft and quiet; conversely, the boys' colors are bold, bright, and strong. If these are the messages we accept for our infants, could this in some way alter the way we treat and parent the different sexes?

Nearly every product relating to infants—from baby shower invites to pacifiers to crib sheets to car seats and strollers—is color coded by gender. The infant clothing sections in the big box shops and mainstream department stores are nearly entirely divided into pink and blue. The divide is so commonplace that people fail to even think about it. In fact, I often hear people argue that babies are biologically predisposed to prefer their assigned colors, never mind that these assignments didn't actually appear in our culture en masse until around 1985. When our grandparents were children, blue was the preferred color for girls, red and pink for boys.

With advances in ultrasound technology, couples can learn the sex of their baby as early as fifteen weeks of gestation. Sure, parents want

> *Creating your baby's nursery is a wonderful experience. To avoid gender stereotypes, try for bright colors with neutral themes such as hot air balloons or kites, vintage storybook characters such as Beatrix Potter, or geometric patterns such as dots and stripes.* ❋

to know the sex of their child to help bond with the baby or ease the stress of pregnancy or to find out if they're finally having a girl after having three boys, and all of those are good reasons. Healthy babies and happy families are what we're after, and if knowing the sex helps your family, then that is great. But I have had more than one friend say they have to "find out what they are having" solely so they know what stuff to buy. What they are really saying is they need to know which colors to buy. This isn't really the fault of the parents, as virtually all baby products are color coded by gender and I'm sure a lot of families feel like they don't want to buy the "wrong color."

But parents who buy into the pink-and-blue divide should realize it has nothing to do with child development and everything to do with marketers wanting to increase consumerism. A 2007 Gallup poll showed that more than 66 percent of parents would want to find out the sex of their unborn child. Companies know this and adjust their products accordingly. Why create and sell one baby item when you can sell the same family both a girl version and a boy version of that item? When families buy color-coded and gender-themed products, they eventually purchase more stuff as they continue to have subsequent children of the opposite sex and thus require the opposite color or theme.

Say you are a family like mine, and you first have a baby girl and then a boy. If my husband and I had found out Amelia's sex before she was born and had received all pink and "feminine" items, how compelled would we have been to then acquire all blue items for our second child, a son? How accepting is our culture of boys draped in pink or flowers? Not very.

The interesting thing is, I have yet to meet a baby who cares what color its clothes and stroller are. If you think about it, most babies are pretty much the same, and have the same needs. Pink or blue is not one of them. Whenever I'm buying a

> Register for your baby online, where stores have a much wider selection and finding gender-neutral items is easier. If you keep the big items gender-neutral, they will accommodate a growing family. ❋

baby gift for a family, I like to put together a themed gift basket (such as safari or farm animals) and include board books and bath toys and a gift certificate to a locally owned clothing store or the Pigtail Pals shop. I try to find items that represent a rainbow of color.

My husband and I did not find out the sex of our children before their births. Both times I was expecting, I was heavily pregnant over Christmas and thought it would be fun to have the doctor write down the sex and seal it in an envelope we could open on Christmas morning. My husband was adamant we wait and be surprised at birth. Looking back, I'm so glad we made this choice. When people heard we were expecting, they would ask what we were having. My answer was always the same: "A small baby." Several people were exasperated with me, saying they had no idea what to buy "it" because they needed to know if it was a boy or girl. I usually replied with something like, "I am so happy about your excitement for the arrival of this child. Children's books and toys would be a wonderful addition to our home."

> To avoid gender stereotypes and set the tone for if and when you find out the sex of your baby, play with fun ways to announce his or her arrival with neutral descriptions such as, "Our little explorer is set to arrive" or "A little creative wonder is cooking." ❀

I've had some friends use very clever ways to announce the arrival of their girls. One friend found out they were having a second daughter and posted a Facebook status update that read, "The Girl Power is about to double in our house! Baby Girl arriving in September!" Another friend announced the arrival of her gorgeous daughter with a birth announcement that read, "There's a new sheriff in town, and she means business!" Both were great ways to set the tone for how they wanted their friends and family to regard the new little girl who had joined their lives. I watched those posts with interest, because most of the comments were about how awesome girls are to raise, how fun it will be to have a girl, how cool girls are, and so on.

On the other hand, I have another friend who announced the impending arrival of her daughter with, "Our world is about to turn pink!" and nearly every single comment was about being excited to meet her "new little princess." This is a great example in the difference between the color pink and "pink culture." I like the color pink. I wear it frequently, as does my daughter. My favorite shoes are fuchsia pink and I've even been known to put dark pink highlights in my hair. But I don't subscribe to pink culture, for me or my daughter. My daughter has never worn a piece of clothing that refers to her as a princess or an entitled shopaholic. We managed to go six years with virtually no Disney princesses or Barbies in our house, we don't refer to her as a "drama queen" or "sassy diva" as if it is something to achieve, and we steer clear of senseless gendered marketing (often called pinkification).

Pink is a lovely color among many to be enjoyed by both boys and girls. Pink culture is an assuming and limiting way to box a little girl into a preconceived notion of what she will like, how she will act, and what she will do. Essentially, pink culture (also called princess culture) tells a girl how to be a female, and the definition is a very narrow one.

From the time she was born, we have never called Amelia "Princess" as a nickname. Store clerks and nurses have, and she has set them straight, since the age of three, astutely correcting them that she is indeed not a princess. She has never liked princesses. We've called her Lia, Chippy, Choodle, "my babes," Pumpkin, Sweetie Bee, Smooch, and for the entire year that she was three years old she demanded she be called Amelia Dinosaur. I call her Smalls because she is my mini-me. My husband calls her Chippy because when she was a baby her laugh sounded like a chipmunk. My dad calls her Beetle because of the way she crawled as an infant. My mom calls her Rascal Pants. Her beloved uncles also call her Smalls, in reference to a great movie character from *The Sandlot*. Her auntie has a South African–Canadian accent and has the most beautiful way of saying "Amelia My Girl." My best friend met Amelia when she was twelve hours old and has always called her Buddy. Her baby brother Benny calls her Nama. Her little cousin calls her Mia. If you were to meet Amelia and mistakenly call her Princess, she would let you know that she is a "science-exploring girl" named after a heroic aviator. If nothing else, I am proud my daughter is not a foregone conclusion.

On the flip side, of all the nicknames we have for her little brother, we've never called him Prince, nor has anyone else. Have you noticed that there is hardly any focus on boys being princes or acting in a princely, gallant manner? In fact, they are told and encouraged to be rowdy, loud, sporty, mischievous, messy monsters.

I'd much rather we let our children define childhood for themselves while we adults take our gender stereotypes, forced upon them before they even take their first breath, and get out of their way.

Letters from the Experts
Veronica Arreola and Family

Veronica Arreola is the director of the UIC Women in Science and Engineering program and owner of *Viva la Feminista*, her blog on which she explores the intersection of motherhood and feminism. Her husband, Tony Martinez, and daughter, Elizabeth, contributed to these letters as well.

✳　✳　✳

Dear Parents,

Some people see me as a girl and expect me to wear pink tutus and go to ballet. But that's not the kind of girl I am. My name is Elizabeth Martinez and I *love* sports. My parents introduced me to soccer right away because I had a powerful kick when I was in my mom's tummy, so try and find something natural in your child. But always remember to remind them to be themselves.

Sincerely,
Elizabeth, age nine

❀ ❀ ❀

Dear Fellow Parents,

We have been working on "redefining girly" in our home for almost ten years. We count this endeavor from the day we found out Veronica was pregnant because, as you may well know, people want to talk about the gender of our children before a penis or vagina even forms on the embryo. It is hard to fight against society's desire to place gender stereotypes on our children, especially before they are even born. At our baby shower, we had two cakes, one pink and one blue. As this is written, the rage is having gender-revealing cakes. A woman's doctor writes down the gender of the baby and the paper is given to the bakery. The cake is made with pink or blue filling inside, so everyone finds out the sex when the woman slices open her cake. *Surprise!* So we understand there's pressure to find out "what" you are having and then operate according to said stereotype.

What we can offer you is what our daughter was trying to convey: Let children be themselves. If they are prone to climbing, let them climb. If they like to play dress up, let them—even if your son is the one who wants to play dress up. The world is a tough and rough place for our kids. They have many pressures, and while it may seem tempting to teach them to hunker down and go with the flow, we believe if we teach them to stand tall and believe in themselves, they will fare much better in life.

Our daughter likes to play soccer; that is a fact. She has a poster of the 2012 gold medal–winning team on her door. Nevertheless, she also likes to dress up. She loves sparkly clothes, but in a punk-rock way. She likes to take time to brush her hair . . . when she wants to. She likes to paint her nails. She's a girly girl who is one of the top goal scorers on her team. She looks good when she climbs trees. She defies both the girly and tomboy stereotypes by embodying them both at the same time.

People like to put kids in boxes, but we all know kids love to climb out of boxes, bust through their thin walls, and with our support, they can do that to the gender boxes too. Come on, be brave! There are more of us out here than you think.

Peace,
Veronica Arreola and Tony Martinez Jr.

How to Start Redefining Girly in Your Home

In the early years of parenthood, we have a lot of control over what our kids are exposed to. As the parent to a small child, you are the authority on what toys, clothes, and media come into your home.

This becomes less true as the children grow and move into their school years (or day care) and as their development shifts and friends replace parents as a central influence. We don't parent in a vacuum: Gender stereotypes and sexualization are going to creep into our home. They are a pestilence. Both elements are part of our culture, as are our children. We cannot escape that culture, but we can be smart parents who raise children who know how to think critically and who will not be defined by it.

Parents never really lose their clout, and children want our guidance, so it is important we stay on top of our game. Even in my house, where my husband and I are vigilant, our kids are not immune to picking things up from our culture that we would prefer they hadn't. Some of the things I hear them parrot drive me up the wall. But I do not feel as though I've failed as a parent or that they have done something wrong; I take it in stride and remember the foundation they are getting at home is what is most important.

When your kids come home saying keen things like, "Pink is only for girls and blue is only for boys" or "I'm going to grow up to be a princess and marry a rich prince and be a mommy," and your *Free to Be . . . You and Me* self is standing there in shock, you keep calm and carry on, as the saying goes. We always say, "Colors are for everyone" at our house. The kids can have their favorite colors, which generally change on a monthly basis, but they are not allowed to limit what someone else may like. Whenever the kids repeat a stereotype, I try to find the positive in their words and work from there. I would respond to the "I want to marry a rich prince" comment with, "Oh, it is so fun to grow up and fall in love with someone special. I love being a mommy, but I also like that I support our family by working and traveling for a job I love. Do you want me to tell you a story about that?" That way you are not making your children ashamed of what they are saying, but rather repackaging it and giving them a wider idea to work with. There is a great amount of power in telling your own stories to challenge what they are absorbing from media and our culture.

As they are sorting out ideas about gender, kids in preschool can be didactic in their statements of what girls and boys can and cannot do. Remember that this is normal and that you have not failed as a parent. They are little people and have a lot to figure out about the world, and the rigidness in stereotypes helps them feel safe. No matter what they say, surely you can come up with a clever quip to gently challenge the stereotype, if nothing else but to earn a "My mom/dad knows nothing" eye roll from your worldly three-year-old.

As for the more eye-popping questions older kids come home with much earlier than you might think, you and your parenting partner need to have a game plan in place for how you will discuss sex, violence, swearing, and body image (more about body image in chapter 6). All of these issues came up for us in kindergarten. I was expecting it to be more like sixth or seventh grade. Get cozy talking about body parts and their functions, and I strongly encourage you to practice using the correct anatomical terms with your children. A penis is a penis and a vulva is a vulva and an elbow is an elbow. Always answer the specific question your child asked, and nothing more. One afternoon Amelia asked me, "Is Daddy neutered, or can he still make babies?" I'm fairly certain she did not have the big picture in mind when asking her question; she only wanted that singular question answered. So I answered it, very matter-of-factly and calmly with "He can still make babies." She had no further questions, as that was all she wanted to know in that minute. I wrapped it up with, "Any time you want to ask me a question, I'll always help you find the answer."

The most important thing is for Amelia to know she can come to me with questions and that she will be treated respectfully and honestly. By answering her calmly and matter-of-factly, I send the message that our bodies and our sexuality are not shameful or embarrassing. Laying this kind of groundwork will repay itself in spades as your daughter gets bigger and comes up with bigger questions. You and your partner need to be her go-to people for information, especially when it involves sex and sexuality.

Your home is your nest, and you get to say what flies or not. You have the chance to lead by example, both with actions and with the words you use. You get to pick your battles and measure out well-rounded and diverse experiences. You instill your family's values. It helps greatly when you have a partner, friend, or other family member who backs you up and supports the idea of a gender-equal home in order to raise empowered girls.

It can feel daunting when your child encounters peers who expose her to things that make you cringe. This past year Amelia really wanted a doll that was overtly sexual and represented a physical figure I find to be damaging to a healthy body image. As much as I wanted to say, "Over my dead body," I knew that would not teach her anything or allow her to make good decisions for herself. Instead I talked to her in an age-appropriate way about why her dad and I thought the doll was inappropriate for kids (more on this in chapter 5), asked her what she liked about the doll, and offered some healthier alternatives. She wasn't happy, but she got the message and made good choices with her alternatives.

Letters from the Experts

Rachel Simmons

Rachel Simmons is an educator and coach who helps girls and young women grow into authentic, emotionally intelligent, and assertive adults. She is the author of *Odd Girl Out: The Hidden Culture of Aggression in Girls* and *The Curse of the Good Girl: Raising Authentic Girls with Courage and Confidence*.

Dear Parents,

I keep a photo of my five-year-old self on my desk. In it, I'm holding a basketball that looks twice as big as my head. I've got pigtails and knee socks, and my T-shirt is tucked into shorts that are hiked way up. All I care about is showing off this big ball in my hands—and what I'm about to do with it. I don't care about what I look like, or what anyone thinks. I'm completely in the moment.

I've devoted my life to helping girls hold on to that kind of unself-conscious joy—the kind that starts to fade as girls approach adolescence and become aware of what society expects a "good girl" to be. When girls start worrying about what others think, they stop speaking their minds. Girls begin to shrink, literally and figuratively.

It is precisely at this moment that a committed parent like you becomes most important. We're pressured to parent from a place of deficit. We wonder if this or that thing we did (or didn't do) is going to screw our kids up. Fighting for your daughter means parenting with positive intention: thinking about the little things you do each day that are giving her the words and permission to be herself. It also means parenting with faith: believing, despite her objections or rolling eyes, that she will draw the benefits later on if not now.

No matter what toxic message your daughter encounters outside of your home, no matter how in love she seems to be with whatever infuriating fad, and no matter how much she acts annoyed when you resist, she is still listening to you. She is watching. And the things you do, especially the small things, count a lot.

My mom used to take my brother and me to a fast food restaurant after school sometimes. She loved ordering french fries, but if they were too cold, she'd ask the fry cook to reheat them. I thought this was humiliating. I begged my mother to stop "being rude" and accept the fries as is. She reminded me she was paying for the fries and had a right to enjoy them hot. Years later, as an adult, I got a plate of lukewarm fries. Without thinking, I asked for them to be reheated. I knew, in that moment, that my mother had given me the personal authority to ask for what I needed—something I watched so many of my female friends struggle with.

Being yourself around your daughter is a revolutionary act. Your everyday, small moments are what she will remember and emulate for years to come. What will be her French fry story? She is lucky to have a parent like you who will give her one.

See you in line for fries,
Rachel Simmons

You are in charge of "corporate communications" for your family. Be clear and firm in your messages to your children. Have family meetings and allow your kids to have a voice. They will test you nine ways from Sunday, but they are listening to you. They want your guidance and need you setting boundaries and holding them to those boundaries. To add to that: You are in charge of your children's media. You decide what comes in and what doesn't, and must help them digest what does come in. Media consumption is like food consumption; it is the responsibility of the parents to set limits and feed their child well. Choose media (this also includes toys, clothing, music, and social media) that honor girlhood, build girls up, show them in positions of leadership and strength, and that do not perpetuate gender stereotypes and sexualization.

Here is a list of things we have done in our home to broaden our children's sense of the world, to make sure Amelia had a well-rounded definition of "girly," and to make it easier for us to teach media literacy:

- ❀ Both my husband and I have fed, changed, bathed, and put our children to bed. Having a "hands-on dad" shows your kids that parenting is a team effort, not just "mom's job." It also teaches them that dads are competent and responsible, since fathers are often portrayed in the media as goofy and childish.
- ❀ Our son is encouraged to play with dolls or stuffed animals and love on them, as this teaches Amelia that Benny is not being "girly" or "gay," he is being a good daddy, just like his daddy is.
- ❀ My daughter sees me mow the lawn and use tools, just like she sees her dad wash dishes, cook, and fold laundry.
- ❀ At family get-togethers, I make sure I am outside playing in the pick-up game of touch football or soccer or building a snow fort. That is not just the "guy's territory," that is fun territory, and I want in.
- ❀ My daughter sees me eat dessert—and enjoy it. No comments about being "bad" or ruining a diet or my hips.
- ❀ We have books everywhere in the house. By the age of two Amelia was a voracious "reader." We keep the children's books

on a low shelf and in cloth cubes on the floor in their rooms. We are regulars at the local library, and I make an effort to find books that equally feature boys and girls in the story lines.

❋ We watch very little television, and what we do watch as a family is usually commercial-free preschool programming, PBS, or a science channel like National Geographic.

❋ We have toy "stations" around the house and we rotate locations. The train table has been in Amelia's room, the toy kitchen in Benny's. The dollhouse is out in the family room, along with blocks, puzzles, cars, and board games. All toys are kept at eye level or lower for the kids and in primary-colored containers that are easy to access.

❋ We turn down hand-me-down toys and clothes that do not fit with our family ideals for our children. We'll say, "Thank you so much for thinking of us" and then politely decline or donate away items that carry messages we feel are not a fit with our family morals.

❋ There is one communal dress-up box, and there are no rules about who wears what. Benny is partial to butterfly wings, Amelia to safety goggles and capes.

❋ We have rainbow-colored cups, bowls, plates, and silverware that are character-free. I pull out whatever color comes first, and you get what you get and you don't throw a fit.

❋ I make sure the entire rainbow is present in my children's closets. There is not a single color that dominates either wardrobe. I also let the children pick their own clothes, as this gives them a sense of power and is good practice in discussions about appropriateness that can transfer over to bigger topics like sexualized clothing.

❋ There are art supplies in two locations that the kids have free access to, minus glue bottles and glitter. Our kitchen table always has a basket of early learning workbooks, blank paper, and drawing/coloring supplies so that at any time they can sit and create. We also have an art center on our back porch, and the kids often use things from nature in their art.

❈ When the kids have a funny idea or story, we'll say something like, "Can you go draw a picture of that for me?" This is the beginning step in teaching kids to create their own media.

❈ Amelia received our old digital camera for her sixth birthday to encourage her to take pictures and make movies. Girls have just as much of a place behind the camera directing and creating as they do in front of it and smiling.

❈ Each parent in our family spends individual time with each child. It can be as simple as taking a walk around the block, running in the big field across the street from our house, reading a pile of books together, or going on a little outing to a craft store or coffee shop. Last summer Amelia's favorite thing to do was put on a hand-me-down flower girl dress and rain boots, while her daddy dressed in a shirt and tie, and the two would walk hand-in-hand to the corner coffee shop to play checkers and Candy Land.

❈ We spend a lot of time outside as a family, usually hiking, biking, playing sports, and visiting local parks.

❈ We have built a playhouse, tree fort, and swing set in our backyard so that the kids can be outside and have a rip-roaring time lost in free play. Sidewalk chalk, bug catchers, and scooters and bikes seem to be everywhere.

❈ We spend time with families who share our values. When questions about differences come up, we answer the kids with facts, absent of judgment toward people who do things differently.

❈ Most important, we talk with our kids and always encourage them to question everything.

Letters from the Experts

Dr. Jennifer W. Shewmaker

Jennifer W. Shewmaker is a nationally certified school psychologist and licensed specialist in school psychology. Dr. Shewmaker is an associate professor of psychology at Abilene Christian University and the author of a forthcoming book about children, sex, and media.

❄ ❄ ❄

Dear Parents,

As a girl, I always felt a bit like I didn't quite fit what I knew was expected of me. As an ambitious, driven, serious student, I didn't fit the ideal for the sweet, nurturing, gentle girl. I went on to pursue my doctorate and establish a professional career. My husband, Stephen, was my main support, both financially and emotionally, throughout my educational and professional career. He always believed in the ability of a woman to be strong, smart, and ambitious. When we became parents of three daughters, we were both determined to help our girls reach their potential and pursue their interests and not be held back because they were girls.

As our oldest daughter reached the age of ten, we became aware of the toxic sexualized messages coming through media and marketing aimed straight at her. We committed to each other and to our daughters that we would do what we could to promote a healthier, broader idea of what it meant to be a girl and a woman.

Through my work as a researcher, writer, and speaker, I share a bigger vision for both girls and boys. All three of our daughters are their own kind of girly. One is analytical and loves math, science, and filmmaking. The second is nurturing and loves all things sparkly and experimenting with fashion, hair, and makeup to express herself. The third is athletic and loves sports, animals, and reading. All are different, and all perfectly amazing girls.

We try to help our girls and other kids develop a bigger vision for themselves through developing relationships with a wide array of role models who show them unique ways of being successful and fulfilled as adults. From organizing STEM (Science, Technology, Engineering, and Math) weekends for middle school girls to visit college campuses and interact with female faculty and students, to working together as the lead room parents in our daughters' classroom, we hope to model a broader vision of what it means to be men and women.

While our thirteen-year-old still gets teased for her love of science and tech, we know we still have work to do. When our eight-year-old is able to finally wear a shirt to school featuring her favorite cartoon character, even though she's been told it's "for boys," we know we're making progress.

We want to redefine girly so that one day those girls who love math and technology, who demonstrate leadership skills, or who are nurturing and gentle, will all feel perfectly comfortable and accepted as girls. We've got a way to go, but we're moving forward, and our family is excited to be a part of that!

The Shewmakers,
Jennifer, Stephen, Rylan, Catherine, and Alexandra

Getting Family and Friends on Board

Growing up, I was that kid who did not have cable, had to tell my mom ahead of time what movie my friends and I were watching at a sleepover, had to discuss with my mom the meaning of lyrics to certain songs, and had to explain to my parents why I wanted to wear an outfit when they did not approve.

I was convinced I had the most unfair parents on earth. Like in fifth grade, when I was the only girl not allowed to watch *Dirty Dancing*, even though all my friends had seen it and thought I was a baby. Or in eighth grade, when I bought a Levi's BUTTON YOUR FLY T-shirt at the mall just like all my friends did (having no idea what the double entendre really meant) and my mom had a long talk with me that night about how we represent ourselves in public and what messages our clothes give about the level of respect we hold for ourselves and want from others.

I can remember feeling exasperated with my parents' "teachable moments." I wanted them, just once, to shrug and say, "Whatever." In hindsight, I am grateful my parents cared about the media and cultural influences my brothers and I were taking in. I am grateful they did not give a resolute "No!" but rather talked with me about my choices and what consequences they might bring. My mom worked as a counselor at our school and saw firsthand the effects of the issues I now talk about with other parents: sexualization, low self-esteem, depression, body image issues, aggression and bullying, promiscuity and slut-shaming. With a culture increasingly sexualizing girlhood (especially clothing), slut-shaming has become a way for girls to police one another by making public comments about the real or perceived sexual history and gender performance of a peer.

I think my mom understood the big picture of what all of these media messages meant to her three kids. Though she never used these terms, she was totally in tune with issues of media literacy, sexualization, and self-esteem. My earliest memory of this was in second grade and her talking about how she found Madonna to be very lacking as a role model. I remember being told that Madonna was "inappropriate." Looking back on it, my mom was trying to find a way to say that Madonna was too sexually charged for children. I now use the word *inappropriate* with my daughter, during discussions about sexually charged performers or products that can be difficult to explain to a young child.

I wondered if my mom's family and friends supported her in her views, and I asked her one day when I was working on this book, "Mom, were the other moms thinking the same way when you were raising me? Or did you feel kind of on your own about this stuff?"

"I felt alone. Your father agreed with it, but most people didn't see the harm and thought I was crazy. They would say it wasn't that big of a deal and that I should lighten up," she answered, her eyes kind of tight, like she was remembering some hurtful conversations.

"I have parents tell me they hear the same things today," I told her. "How did you know it was the right thing to do?"

"How does a parent *not* know?" Mom replied. "Young girls dressing in a sexy manner was just, well, it is dangerous for them because they don't understand what it is they are advertising and they don't understand what it does to them emotionally. It was just too much, too soon. Madonna, she was a real piece of work. I hated Barbie, but you kept getting them for gifts. I never bought you a Barbie. I took a lot of crap from the family, saying I was too uptight and needed to relax. I was made fun of for it. But I knew how I wanted to raise you." My mom stated this with great resolve.

I was impressed. "But how did you know it would be so important?" I asked. "Did you feel like you were ahead of your time?"

"Sweetheart, I don't know. It just seemed like common sense. We didn't have cable until after you graduated high school, and that helped. God, MTV was awful. We spent more family time with the people who understood. And you stayed busy with sports and school and babysitting. I do remember feeling like I had to be the media police and feeling out of sync with many of my peers. I just remember thinking little kids shouldn't have to be thinking about this stuff."

I would love to see her notes from when I was a kid in the 1980s, during the deregulation of children's advertising and before sexualization became mainstream in childhood. Looking back, things seemed a lot simpler when I grew up. It would be fascinating to compare them to the feelings parents have about the issues we face now.

> Remember that you are not alone or crazy for seeing problems with the emotionally toxic ways our culture treats girls. The Resources section at the end of this book is full of alternatives, information, and the names of experts who can help. Our daughters deserve a girlhood free of harm and limitations. ❋

How many times have you felt the way my mom was feeling, when she was being questioned for wanting healthy media for her children? It can be difficult when you are the only one in your extended family or group of friends to challenge the status quo. I have had people tell me they feel like they are in the twilight zone when they are the only one in a group who is aware of how sexualization and gender stereotypes can limit our kids. It can feel frustrating and downright hurtful when your family does not back you up or intentionally undermines your efforts to give your daughter a healthy girlhood.

I had a parent tell me, "Unfortunately I know several moms and family members who think several products I feel sexualize children are fine and *I'm* the one who's weird, too strict, and overprotective for keeping this trash out of my daughters' lives. I'll happily take any of those labels."

I believe most families want to raise their daughters with self-respect, a desire for knowledge and learning, a healthy sense of their body and their sexuality, and pride from meaningful achievements. There are some universal truths to parenting, the first being: we want happy, healthy kids. I believe that pushback from other people is a manifestation of their willful denial of the issues, specifically when parents like me want to rock the boat. When we do things differently it forces others to look at and question the cultural norms they are accepting, and that can be uncomfortable for them. The status quo that sells girls short is interwoven with longstanding fairytales steeped in tradition, a largely unquestioned standard of beauty, long-ingrained and internalized sexism and sexualization, and the patriarchal weight of many generations. It can be unsettling for people to question all of this, especially if "all of this" is all they have ever known or been told.

I tell parents all the time, "Once you see it, you cannot unsee it."

> Part of parenthood is dealing with everybody else's opinions on how you are doing your job. It helps to have a prepared response to criticism of your viewpoint, such as "Thank you for your advice" or "Our family has chosen this approach" or "I really appreciate your input and will consider it as I continue learning." ❋

Seeing "it" everywhere only deepens your resolve as you grow increasingly puzzled and even frustrated by the people who are blind to it or, worse, intentionally ignorant and participating in it. When these people are your family members or close friends—people you love—it can be doubly painful and tricky trying to discuss these issues. You want to convey how important these concerns are without coming off as judgmental or belittling, and you have to be sensitive to family politics as you do it.

The relationships your children have with your extended families and friends are important, because it truly does take a village to raise a child and these are people who care about your children. It would be nice if they also shared your same values, but for a lot of folks this kind of thinking is rather new. Just like with any other change to social norms, whether it be wearing seat belts in automobiles, installing smoke detectors in homes, or advertising the health risks of cigarette smoking, true change takes time and a whole lot of education. Of course, all of those initiatives were eventually backed by federal and state laws. Maybe one day we'll have our chance and marketing products and media known to be harmful to children will be regulated or come to a stop.

Until that time, parents need a practical tool kit of responses to help express to those around them that their family does not participate in sexualization and gender stereotypes. I have found there are gentle and respectful ways to try to educate others without coming off as draconian or obnoxious. The truth is, research study after study backs up what we know and how we feel about sexualization and gender stereotypes and how they affect our kids, so it has always felt comforting to me that this isn't an opinion or trend (or me being crazy), it is peer-reviewed science in the fields of child development, marketing, and psychology.

Here are some ways to deal diplomatically with criticism of your views:

❋ Have a prepared team response you and your parenting partner will use that lets family know this is an issue you take seriously and that you want to have your wishes respected. My husband and I use, "We want Amelia to be happy and healthy and we feel this is the best path to achieve that." (We use the same message for our son.)

❀ Have fun alternatives ready to suggest to family and friends who bring media into your home that you feel are unhealthy. This way you are not just saying no to their media, rather, you are saying yes to healthier choices.

❀ Have a secret signal for your kids to use so they can communicate to you that they need to ask you a question or talk to you about something later (like a baseball coach signal—helpful when a gift is given or a comment is made that your kids know goes against what you teach at home).

❀ Have a conversation starter and closer at the ready. This will help you speak up when you need to and wrap things up when the discussion has run its course. I tend to use, "I need to mention something to you about . . ." and "I really appreciate you listening to what I had to say." This allows you to advocate for your child, respect the other person's point of view, and walk away in a mutually respectful manner while still sticking to your way of parenting.

❀ There are some popular one-liners in the Pigtail Pals community that have actually been turned into T-shirt designs because they speak our truth and really pack a punch: "Colors are for everyone," "Pretty's got nothing to do with it," "There are many ways to be a girl/boy," and "Toys are made for kids, not genders." These lines are easy to remember and to the point. They are particularly helpful when you hear a very sexist or homophobic comment made toward your child.

The trick is to focus on what you *do* want for your daughter rather than sheltering her from everything you don't want. Communicate to others what you do appreciate and approve of, instead of condemning what you do not.

Family Affairs

As a parent, advocating for your child is a lifelong commitment. Parents-to-be learn that this starts immediately. Everyone—most of all members of your family—has an opinion about whether or not you should find out or share the unborn baby's sex, potential names, nursery colors, birth plan, and so forth. Their excitement over welcoming a new little one may lead them to believe that you want them to openly share all of their opinions on how you should birth, love, and raise your child. Get very good at smiling and saying, "Thanks for your input." The outsider op-eds will continue as your child grows.

Family members mean well. They are excited for the arrival of the baby and want to celebrate by connecting to the child. Even though most of the hopes and dreams your family is forming around your baby can and should be the same whether it is born a boy or girl, you'll undoubtedly hear remarks about taking the grand*son* fishing, or sewing princess dresses for a darling girl. Both of those would make for fine memories for a child, but why not take the opportunity to get those more traditional relatives to think outside the gender box that will limit your child? Set the tone of the conversation for your family by focusing on the wonderful childhood memories and family traditions that make up the fabric of your story. A few examples:

> "Uncle Chuck and I still have our secret fishing spot. I think we'll have to show this little one where it is as soon as she is big enough to hold a fishing rod."

> "Do you remember the puppet shows we used to do, Aunt Nancy? It will be so fun to watch this baby grow and play with Jill's children the way we used to play when we were kids."

> "We were thrilled to find out the girls will be identical twins. That will make it easier to plan trick plays with them during the Thanksgiving flag football game because we all know how Uncle Bernie and Eric love to cheat."

When you take the lead and set the tone with your own hopes and dreams for your children, others become aware of the story you have begun to tell for your child. Because your child will be preverbal for the first year to two of life, you will be her storyteller. There are no limits to how you craft the story around your baby learning about the world.

While I was pregnant I told my mother-in-law the child would be named Amelia Joyce, "after Amelia Earhart and my mother," if born a girl. I remember her letting out a happy sigh and saying it was a good name for a strong and smart girl. It definitely helped us to set the tone for how we wanted people to treat her.

I mentioned earlier that my dad calls my daughter Beetle. Amelia had begun to crawl between visits

> My experience has been that success comes not from trying to change people's minds or getting them to leave behind an old way of thinking, but rather in helping them buy into a healthier way of looking at our girls. ❋

to the grandparents' house, and I remember bragging to my dad about what an expert, athletic crawler my six-month-old was. I intentionally focused on what she was doing and how she was doing it, rather than how she looked while doing it. I did not mention how cute she looked while crawling, instead saying I thought she demonstrated solid potential to become a ninja. He said he didn't believe me; she couldn't be crawling yet, and he would have to see my champion crawler for himself. During our next visit, he was impressed with how adept Amelia was at measuring up and working her way through a room, usually navigating underneath, around, or through furniture at freakishly fast speeds. She became the Beetle.

Begin to tell your child's tale to your friends and family during the years she cannot yet speak for herself, and as you do this, speak your truth. You control how you shape your comments around media, toys, and body image as they relate to your daughter. You can steer talk to focus on her abilities, skills, and achievements and deepen the conversation beyond

"Oh, she's so cute!" Of course she's cute, she's a little kid. Encourage people to see her for more than just a precious little face.

Try some of these:

"Oh, Grandma, I think you should come watch our little mathematician count and sort her Goldfish crackers. Look at her concentration!"

"Yes, we do love Cora's cute, round tummy. She fills it up with healthy food and it is helping her to grow so big and strong."

"We certainly appreciate Angelina's birthday gift. Thank you for celebrating with us. Maybe we'll take the Barbie out of the box in a bit, but right now Angelina is really content building with her blocks and dominoes. Lina really does build some of the best skyscrapers around."

"My goodness, how fancy Auntie Jenn made you look while Mommy was at the store! That makeup lets you look very grown-up. Was it fun to play dress up with Auntie? Just remember that before we leave for the park, we need to clean up our dresses and makeup and get back to natural beauty time."

It is oftentimes a steadfast habit for people to compliment a girl on her looks. As Lisa Bloom pointed out in a *Huffington Post* blog entry from 2011, "How to Talk to Little Girls":

I always bite my tongue when I meet little girls, restraining myself from my first impulse, which is to tell them how darn cute/pretty/ beautiful/well-dressed/well-manicured/well-coiffed they are.

What's wrong with that? It's our culture's standard talking-to-little-girls icebreaker, isn't it? And why not give them a sincere compliment to boost their self-esteem? Teaching girls that their appearance is the first thing you notice tells them that looks are more important than anything.

In the piece, Bloom goes on to describe the conversation she had with the little girl about books (both the reading and writing of them), friendships, and favorite colors. This really resonated with me, as I can remember being in junior high and high school and the first interactions I had with relatives when we were visiting them in Toledo typically went like this: "Well, hi there, Missy! You are looking prettier and prettier each time we see you. How is school going? Do you have a boyfriend?"

I would take a deep breath and pause. Being told I was pretty did not feel like a compliment, because I didn't have anything to do with it. And the boyfriend question really only seemed to be a further validation of my prettiness. At this age, I was able to tell my own story and speak my own truth. "Nope," I would say, "no time for the dumb boys I know because I've got to keep up my GPA, play on the soccer/volleyball/basketball team, serve as an officer for student council, practice the flute, and babysit."

By the time I was finishing high school and moving into my college years, my extended family realized I had no interest in or time for a steady boyfriend and began to ask me questions about my studies and my activities. It felt great to be recognized for my achievements and experiences.

My immediate and extended family have always been supportive of girls excelling in school, playing in sports, being leaders in extracurricular activities, and heading off to college. I always felt supported in that regard. I feel like I grew up not confined to gender stereotypes or limitations from my family.

While certainly gender stereotypes are ingrained, especially in older generations, we are the children of the *Free to Be . . . You and Me* era, and we grew up largely free of the gender division we are seeing now for our children. Sometimes waxing nostalgic can help others see how silly things have become. As so many toys have received sexy makeovers, for example, sometimes the best way to get your message across is by making a joke about how much things have changed. Classic toys such as Polly Pocket, Strawberry Shortcake, My Little Pony, and Care Bears have been vamped up and do not look like the versions we grew up with. Your aunt may remember growing up with Astronaut Barbie in the 1960s—and back then a woman in that role would have been groundbreaking. But Barbie several generations later is quite different. When I go shopping today the Barbie dolls that I see in the toy aisle are dressed to go clubbing, get married, or be a princess. Making a joke at Barbie's expense about how much she has changed over the years might help you to steer your aunt toward buying something more appropriate for your little girl.

Whether your child is the first grandchild or the twentieth, she has the right to be an individual and enjoy a healthy childhood. This can be tricky to navigate at extended-family gatherings, though, if her cousins are treated differently. How to approach this with tact? Here are a few ideas:

"Why, Miss Lucy, thank you for bringing Baby Clara your princess heels. But you know, she's just learning to walk. Can you take off your fancy shoes and help teach Clara to walk with her piggy toes?"

"OK, girls, it is almost time for Madeline's nap. I bet she would think it is fantastic if you all got down and crawled with her, like dragons. Who can make the best dragon noise?"

"My loves, we've been outside playing fashion models all morning. My legs are telling me that I need a walk. Who would like to help me push the twins in the stroller and go on a nature hike around the neighborhood? Why don't you grab a bag in case we find some interesting bugs or leaves that we want to bring home and inspect?"

"You know, Anna, Skylar doesn't really know much about downloading music, but I can tell that you do! I know that Skylar loves playing with you so much! Do you have that awesome karaoke app that lets you film the song? We should make some videos and then she could watch them on her tablet on the drive home."

You are also a role model to your nieces and nephews and need to respect how they are being raised. You will have a more lasting impact on your niece if you support her and at the same time widen her ideas of what it means to be a girl than you would by telling her princesses are ridiculous or her music icon is a packaged sex object. Notice that in all of the examples above, the attention shifted to the girls becoming or doing something else, usually an activity that encouraged gross motor skills and exploration. There is no need to put down to children something they love. Instead, use creativity to have them think critically about how something could be just a little bit different and still be really fun.

Whether you see extended family on a weekly basis or just on big holidays, remember that what transpires in your own home is really what will have a lasting impact on your child. When I was addressing this topic on my blog, I wrote about my love of Rice Krispies bars when I was a child. My mom was a health food nut, so she never made them for us, but my best friend's mom, Mrs. Krock, regularly had them for us after school. They were divine, and when I went over to my friend Kelly's house I would devour the huge squares. Yet, to this day, I have never made them as an adult. As much as I loved them as a kid and couldn't wait to go back to Kelly's and eat more of them, the eating habits my mom taught me over the years had a more lasting impact than Mrs. Krock's droolworthy Rice Krispies bars. The point is, periodic exposure to a toy or type of play you are not crazy about is not going to undo the foundation that you have given your child. The exposure will also give you talking points and ways to have meaningful discussions with your children.

Staying on Friendly Terms with Friends

Occasional clashes with extended family are one thing, but working out issues with other families and friends your child sees on a regular basis is another. The fact is, we all have our quirks and do things differently. Sometimes you can work around those differences while still respecting and enjoying one another, and other times you need to take different paths. Cutting ties with harmful friends is just as important as making lasting relationships with the good ones.

I have a close friend whose daughter is a good playmate for Amelia. My friend's little girl is darling, spunky, and loves performance art. She seems to be too young to be boy crazy; nevertheless she is obsessed with Justin Bieber and has been since the age of four. My daughter really has no idea who the Biebs is. In this regard, the girls and the media they take in are very different. While their family does some things differently than ours, they have known my children all of their lives and would be the first people on our doorstep if we had an emergency.

Do I care that their daughter is completely gaga over a teen heart-throb when she is only seven years old? Maybe a little bit, but I recognize that this is less about romantic infatuation and more about hero worship and love of performing. (Justin Bieber is a solid performer, I'll give him that.) I focus on the big picture of the girls' friendship, which is that they play very nicely together and really draw out each other's strengths. Because of this little girl's love of show business, my daughter gets to enjoy music and practice singing and playing in front of a microphone, which helps her fight her massive stage fright. And because of Amelia's love of nature and exploring, the girls are frequently found outside getting filthy while conducting a science experiment that always seems to involve mud.

Friendship requires give and take. And when you are dealing with someone else's kid, it also requires a lot of respect. We've had some playmates over to the house who have done things that have needed redirection. Gentle reminders that in our house, the television does not need to be on during playdates, we eat healthy foods between meals, we keep our clothes on while outside on the swings, and so on is all it takes to let the little friend know our family rules while not making her feel embarrassed or insulted. As Amelia has gotten older, I really try to leave the kids alone and let them figure things out for themselves, especially as Amelia is quite articulate and can repeat our family rules when needed.

Other times, I've had to step in. One playmate insisted that Amelia's little brother could not play with the toy kitchen during a make-believe game of restaurant because "boys cannot cook." I started the conversation with, "All of the toys in our house are for all of the kids," and when that made no headway, I asked some gentle questions to the playmate to get her to think critically, such as: "Why couldn't a boy cook if he has two hands and can read recipes?" I reminded the friend that both her daddy and Amelia's daddy help cook dinners. When I could see the window in her mind opening, I grabbed a cookbook from the shelf that showed men cooking, and it was agreed upon that Benny would be allowed to work as a line cook but the girls would remain the head chefs.

I was not interested in telling the little girl she was wrong or scolding her. I wanted to change the way she could look at something by:

1. Stating our family rules and practices.
2. Asking critical-thinking questions that directly challenge the stereotypes the child has learned without directly challenging the child.
3. Using tangible examples from the house to show that maybe my suggestion isn't completely crazy.

Whenever I do have to step in during a playdate, I try to casually mention the incident to the other parent when the friend is going home. Something simple like, "The girls had so much fun playing together. They played with the dogs, then we colored, and then we all ended up playing restaurant. It was nice of the girls to include Benny in their game, and we learned that boys can be great cooks, too. Thanks so much for letting us spend time with Ellie today!"

It has been my experience—whether you are dealing with a sister, a sister-in-law, or a playmate's parent whom you do not see eye to eye with—that we are all experiencing the same things in parenthood. So while I'm telling my friend's daughter that boys can cook, she may very well have been telling my daughter last week that colors are for everyone. I really appreciate the village around my children, the people who teach them and love them, and I know that we respect one another for both our similarities and our differences.

A big difference that can come up with children playing together is in the types of toys and media found in the family home. I talk about toys in more depth in chapter 5, but here I'll look at how to navigate the relationships those toys can affect.

I firmly believe that highly stereotyped and sexualized toys and images are unacceptable for children. More than likely, the children in your child's group of friends will have such toys and access to such images, because they are in the mainstream and not enough parents are questioning them. While I think it is important to align family relationships with people who share your values, I also believe ending a friendship over a collection of inappropriate toys is silly. My own family looks for other families that are well rounded, show one another respect, and have bright, active, imaginative children. We look for families that respect childhood and don't let their young children behave like teenagers. We are blessed to have an amazing group of friends, doubly important because my children do not have extended family close by. Like most groups of friends, we don't always agree on things, but we seem to align on the big issues and the little stuff we disagree on is OK because we have enough respect for one another to accept the differences.

My friends know that I have strong opinions on these matters. It was interesting for me to make friends with the moms of Amelia's kindergarten playmates. This was a whole new group of families for us, and I was a little anxious about how we would fit in. Coincidentally, the day Amelia started kindergarten was the same day Pigtail Pals had a couple of big events and my name was all over the local and national news for a month or so. In the same week I challenged a sexist T-shirt sold by JCPenney and launched my own T-shirt with a positive counter message for girls. I also wrote a blog post called "Waking Up Full of Awesome" about the self-confidence and positive body image little girls naturally possess. Both events went viral, and by mid-September our reputation preceded us, which made me nervous as to how these new families would perceive us.

One night I was dropping off a new friend of Amelia's after a Girl Scouts meeting and the girls scampered downstairs to play while the mom and I chatted. There was a large Barbie Dream House and about a dozen Barbie dolls in the toy room, and the girls were playing with them and having a grand time. I am no fan of Barbie, but I didn't say anything as I approached the girls, except maybe to ask if they were having fun. Ironically, I had just been on the evening news the night prior, talking about sexualized dolls and little girls' body image. The mom immediately apologized for the Barbie dolls and jokingly asked me not to get mad. I told her I wasn't mad at all and that it was nice to see the girls having fun. I may have certain rules and practices in my home, but I'm not about to impose them while a guest in someone else's home. The girls are still great friends, and the mom is one of my closest friends. It would be foolish to let a collection of twelve-inch plastic dolls get in the way of that!

Experiences like this also give me and my daughter teachable moments. Whether discussing an inappropriate movie, toy, or borrowed outfit from a friend, this is when we have a little face time and talk about what piqued her interest, what our family values are, and how those values measure up to the media messages being given.

We have distanced our family from friends whose children were into nothing but gun play after my own kids expressed discomfort with the level of violence the kids were mimicking. By the same token, while tolerating playdates for years at a house overrun with several forms of media and toys I find objectionable, I finally pulled the plug after the kids put on a fashion show and the little hostess told my then-preschool-aged daughter to "walk sexy because boys will want to get with you." I felt it was time for us to focus on other friendships.

I have a friend who was having trouble with another mother who was repeatedly disrespectful of my friend's parenting and of her daughter. The two women were close friends who had daughters just two weeks apart, and they soon learned that they had very different attitudes about raising girls. She relates that their clashes began at birth and only grew worse over time: "At the age of three I put my girl in karate. I cannot even begin to tell you how much crap I got from her because I didn't put her in dance and that I'm teaching her to 'fight.' It got to the point that I would ignore phone calls, texts, and playdate requests. It was horrible because we had been friends for years before we had kids. I was facing the loss of a friendship. By the time my daughter was five, I had cut ties with her."

Being part of a large group of friends or living in a small community can make it feel risky to take a stand for your kids. There is a lot to consider before you distance or end a friendship, and sometimes this can be avoided by changing the types of activities you do when spending time together. If you do not approve of the toys or media at a friend's house, offer to have park playdates or take bike rides instead. Part of being an adult is respecting differences in others and acting as a dependable, trustworthy friend. Part of being a parent is surrounding your family with people who demonstrate respect toward your children. Finding balance between those two responsibilities is the key.

Stepparents and Coparents

No relationship benefits from balance and respect more than that between parents and stepchildren, stepparents, or coparents. When you become involved with or married to a person who has a child, that child is a part of your relationship. I am a stepparent. I was twenty-two and my stepson was nine when we came into each other's lives. Because he lived in Texas and at that time my husband and I lived in California, where my husband was stationed with the navy, we only got to see him a few times a year. I have a lot of respect for his mother and stepfather and the job they did raising him. My stepson studies at Dartmouth, so he's all grown up and a fine young man. If there were a catalog of stepkids and I got to pick one out, he would have been my first choice.

It isn't always so easy, and many parents write to me asking for advice on how to navigate the intersections of coparenting, stepparenting, and sexualization. The most common question is, How do you succeed when not all sides see the situation the same way?

My answer is to focus not on the other party but on the example that *you* can set, and give voice to your values and expectations. In addition, try not to psychoanalyze your ex (or the new stepparent or significant other), throw out clothes or toys from their home that do not fit your guidelines, or make demands that your rules be honored in their home. To the child, it will appear to be a very fine line between you attacking the negative media and attacking her other parent.

My bottom line is this: Their house, their rules. Your house, your rules.

Coparenting expert Deesha Philyaw, coauthor of *Co-Parenting 101: Helping Your Children Thrive in Two Households After Divorce*, says, "When coparents and stepparents don't agree on what products and media are appropriate for children to consume, we can treat this like an opportunity and a teachable moment, instead of a battle to be won. We can articulate our values and teach our children that reasonable people can disagree about what's appropriate or best, and that people we love can have different values from ours."

With blended families two issues can arise: big age gaps between children and conflicting influences that affect half-siblings and step-siblings. Let's start with the age gaps first. Older stepchildren can be an enormous blessing to a family, as they often become great role models for their younger step- or half-siblings. Such is the case for my family, as my stepson is a state swimming champ and National Merit Scholar. He has five younger half-siblings and is revered as a demigod by all of them. As any parent of young children knows, an extra set of hands to help with wrangling never hurts, and sometimes it is nice to hang out with your kid and not have to watch *Yo Gabba Gabba!*

> It is OK to set boundaries and, frustrating as it may be, not have both parents on the same page. The game plan goes like this: *Their house, their rules. Your house, your rules.* ❋

Conflict can arise when the interests of older children might be appropriate for their age but not for the younger kids in the house. Just like with siblings with large age gaps, striking balance will win the day. Take interest and invest some time in getting to know more about what the older child is into. You may abhor Nicki Minaj, the Snapchat app, and the *Twilight* franchise, but figure out why they appear cool to your kid. Become familiar with the starting lineup for a favorite sports team and who they play in their division, the season's fashion trends, or top video games. This doesn't mean you approve of everything, but it helps you peek into youth culture and speak the native language.

This also gives you the chance to bring up some critical thinking questions, perhaps such goodies as why does an entertainer with any real vocal talent need to twirl sparkly candy on her breasts while performing in a cloud of cotton candy? Other popular points of discussion are the meaning of song lyrics, the off-field behavior of athletes, apparel choices and exposed body parts of celebrities, or maybe the objective of a video game versus the level of violence committed while playing.

Once you better understand the "why" of what your stepkids are into, the next step is explaining to them why the little ones in the house have a different tone to their media and enlisting their help in your efforts:

"Lexi, I know that your music helps you with homework, but I don't want Serena repeating those lyrics at middle school. If I get you an iTunes gift card, would you create a separate playlist for her to listen to when you let her listen to your iPod?"

"Hayley and Brenna, I'm really looking forward to our movie night, but we need to wait until the younger girls are in bed. Our movie choice isn't appropriate for them. Would you two walk the dogs while I put them down? Then we can make our snacks and snuggle in!"

"Frankie, I know you and your dad have talked about this video game and the violence in it, but I am not comfortable with Morgan and Emily watching you play it. They are so much younger than you and don't understand it the way you do. Can you help me think of a way that you can get playtime that doesn't include little eyes watching you?"

There is also the issue of a stepchild bringing media into the home that you feel are inappropriate, no matter her age. It becomes sticky because the child's biological parent has different rules than you do.

My suggestion is to have the child's biological parents find a workable solution. For example, your spouse and the other biological parent can discuss the issue, decide what is appropriate for each household, and come up with a system for respecting and maintaining those boundaries. Your ex doesn't necessarily have to agree with your choices, but he or she needs to respect them as a coparent.

For example, let's say your stepdaughter is allowed by her biological mom to watch movies and wear outfits you feel are sexualizing and unsuitable for a child her age. First, you and your spouse should discuss the issue to ensure you're on the same page. Next, communicate as a team of parents (in the best-case scenario) what the different expectations are for each home. If the other party is unwilling to discuss the issue, then you and your spouse should communicate directly to the child what can and cannot go on in your own home. This may mean asking the child to leave specific items at the other home before she comes to stay at yours. This may also mean keeping a separate wardrobe for her that does not travel between the two houses. This way, the girl is dressed appropriately for family time and follows the rules you have established in your home.

Both sets of parents can mutually respect each other (fake it if you have to) while simultaneously holding different rules or values. One Pigtail Pals reader advised, "You should never try to compete with your stepdaughter's biological mother, nor should you underestimate the connection between the two. But that does not mean you can't have a profound influence purely by being a woman who is not a victim of oversexualized, demeaning messages. By representing what you view as valuable in womanhood, in personhood, to your stepdaughter and to your biological children, you are doing the best you can to show them the potential they have as girls and women-to-be. What they do

> *Every stepparent has a different level of involvement with the kids, but whatever that level is, every stepparent can model for the children involved what kind of adult we want them to grow into.* ✳

or say now does not necessarily represent what they internalize, and the wider the options presented to them in their girlhood, the more likely they are to feel free to choose their own path in adulthood."

More Real-World Examples

Many Pigtail Pals parents have shared their stories about getting their families and friends to buy into their efforts to raise kids free of gender stereotypes and sexualization.

One mother recalled an excursion to the pool with her two daughters, ages two and five, and some other young relatives in their early twenties. "I had to ask the young women to stop referring to themselves as 'fat' in front of my girls," she wrote. "They didn't realize that what they were saying could have a negative impact on my girls, but now they understand. I hope it will help them if and when they have little girls of their own someday."

Another parent wrote to me upset that her daughter, after spending two weeks at her grandmother's house with unlimited access to television (sharply restricted in her own home), came home with an entirely new outlook. The mother wrote, "She is six years old and has always been confident about her appearance, even wearing outrageous clothing that she enjoys putting together. Since she got back from this visit, she has been talking about her belly being too fat and about how she hates her hair. This morning she changed her clothes over and over, crying that nothing looked 'cute.' I am devastated and really want to help her work through this!"

In response I suggested she have an open talk with Grandma about what is and is not appropriate for her daughter to watch while at her house. (Literally, give Grandma a list of channels and shows that are OK, or just tell her no TV at all and send a stack of DVDs next time). I also tried to reassure this anxious mother that two weeks with Gram would not undo six years of healthy parenting and advised her to counter her daughter's negative self-talk with the messages she has been teaching her all along: "So when she says her belly is too fat, don't gasp and ask how she could say that about herself. Instead say something like, 'That is an interesting thing to say. Your doctor and I think your belly is just perfect for your healthy body.'"

I also think she should be honest with her girl about why she is concerned, saying something like, "You know, when you left for Grandma's house you were full of awesome, now I hear you saying things that are hurtful and mean toward your body. Why has that change happened? Because you look exactly the same as when you left. What can we do to work as a team to get back to the awesome?" She could talk about why her daughter's belly looks the way it does (healthy kids don't look like TV stars, because TV stars are handpicked and then coached to look a very certain, narrow way), ask her what she hates about her hair, ask her what makes a cute outfit.

When you hear your daughter making negative comments about her appearance, particularly in response to media she's consuming, try to understand and draw out as best you can what she is thinking. Another idea is to fight the "fun" of the junk TV with the fun of making your own memories with her and instilling your own values surrounding self-care and what is "beautiful." Ask her if she would like to play salon some night and have fun trying out new hairstyles, followed by a bubble bath and some stories. Maybe she can even have a fruit smoothie while soaking in the suds. Or ask if she'd like help putting together outfits from her closet that flatter her body type and bring out her best self.

Another example of getting family on board comes from a Pigtail Pals parent who wrote that her mother won a "girls" gift basket chock-full of Bratz dolls (overtly sexual, heavy-makeup-wearing cousins of Barbie), among other things, at a church raffle. She planned to give the prize to her four-year-old granddaughter. This parent echoed many when she asked, "What do I do? My mom doesn't get it; she thinks every parenting choice I make is nutty. At the same time, she truly has a good heart, gives so much to us, and helps me out in many ways. I really love my mom and I love that she has a close relationship with my kids. But I don't want those stupid dolls anywhere near my daughter."

My response to this concerned parent? "Stick to your guns without offending your well-meaning mama. You could say something like,

'Nana, it is really so sweet of you to think of Avery. We're going to keep the markers from the prize basket, but actually John and I have discussed it, and the sexy dolls for Avery make us uncomfortable. We know how much you cherish Avery and want what is best for her, so thank you for respecting our decision.' Then, quickly redirect the conversation to something positive: 'Oh look, I found this neat pattern online for paper dolls. I'd love it if you and Avery spent some special time together cutting them out and decorating them with the markers from her basket.'"

Letters from the Experts

Rosalind Wiseman

Rosalind Wiseman is an expert on children, teens, parenting, bullying, social justice, and ethical leadership and the author of *Queen Bees and Wannabes* and *Masterminds and Wingmen*.

Dear Parents,

It is way easier said than done. You've done the homework and you believe in your heart and mind about the importance of educating your daughter on the media and its messages to girls that so often are a direct threat to her emotional and physical well-being. And then it happens: your first moment (to be followed by many more) when you need to say something to family members, neighbors, friends, people in the supermarket—who all think that these girly images are so cute and harmless. All of a sudden you feel like you're the uptight girl in high school who was always talking about some terrible thing or injustice and who no one took seriously.

No one wants to be the uptight girl. But I'd like you think about it in a different way. It isn't uptight to know how your daughter is being manipulated by the media. Be proud that you're joining many other people who care about girls and who empower you to be confident and articulate.

But you do have to prepare. Don't wait until the moment it's actually happening to think of what to say. I know you want what's best for her. I am asking you to think about it this way: We want her growing up to believe there's more to her than being cute. So compliment her on something she's specifically doing that you think is great. Ask friends for their support because you'll be raising your girls together. To strangers, I'd say, "Thanks, but you know what's the coolest thing about her? She draws animals incredibly well!" Yes, the other person may think you're strange for saying something so random, but your daughter will hear you complimenting something she specifically does, bringing attention to a skill that you admire. She'll know that the most important people in her life value her for more than her appearance.

This is messy stuff and you don't have to fight every single battle that comes your way. If you're too tired to have these conversations on a particular day, don't sweat it. You'll always have another day! But be proud that you're taking this on. I see way too many girls whose parents haven't provided this guidance and support and truly believe their self-value is based on looking like the "perfect girl." Those girls lose themselves so easily. You take this on, and your daughter will know where you and she stand. Proud. For the right reasons.

Good luck and best wishes,
Rosalind Wiseman

Encouraging Kids at Play—
The Diverse Toy Box

Media greatly influence children, taking a role in shaping their perceptions and behaviors, and toys are a form of media. Just like the healthy foods we feed our children, toys, too, should be "nutrient rich," allowing free play, creativity, and exploration in order to boost brain development and self-esteem through play. There should be no room in the toy box for gender stereotypes and sexualization.

If you were to ask parents, most would say they would do anything for their child. A follow-up question about whether children should be raised free of the limitations of gender stereotypes might not get such a universally affirmative answer. Or maybe the initial response would be positive, but an examination of the clothing and toys in the home might reveal there are different behaviors taking place. As parents, we have to ask ourselves what lessons about gender our children are learning from their toys? The fact that I could have titled this chapter "You

Can Have Anything You Want So Long as It Is Pink" might give us the answer.

It has been a challenge during the first eight years of my daughter's life to find toys for her that reinforce our family's values. I have never seen an Amelia Earhart doll in a store, but I've seen entire rows of highly sexualized dolls, fashion and jewelry design kits, and the like in store after store. What do these teach girls about being female? And why are there so few affordable options to counterbalance those messages? Not only do mainstream stores tout stereotyped toys segregated by gender, the same holds true for television commercials and catalogs that come in the mail, especially around the holidays. Toys are not meant to teach children about gender. They are meant to teach children about life. For the first many years of childhood, I don't see the need for these lessons to be different for boys and girls. As a culture, we are doing a very poor job of establishing a marketplace that reflects what we want our children to learn about being people. As it stands, we are teaching them that girls should focus on beauty and boys should focus on war.

In one of my favorite books, *The Case for Make Believe: Saving Play in a Commercialized World* by Susan Linn, she talks about the need for true pretend play, in which kids are the authors of their stories. Linn describes play as "an essential building block for living a meaningful life." She talks about observations made by her and her colleagues that many children no longer know how to play creatively. Children are born ready to play; it is a skill that comes naturally to them and impacts their cognitive, social, and emotional health. Children have the ability to create entire worlds no one else can see. They can turn nothing into something. My four-year-old son currently turns his hands into people, jets, and animals and will play with his hands acting as puppets for thirty minutes or more. Play has power.

We all hear parents say that children are growing up too quickly these days and wishing kids would just be allowed to be kids. They are right. Highly stereotyped and sexualized products and marketing rush our kids into looking and acting like mini-adults, but at the same time kids are given very little autonomy to wander around the neighborhood and play or to develop responsibilities. This is a generation of helicopter parents and "prosti-tots," and the two ideas together baffle me. We don't think twice about filling an auditorium to cheer wildly as little girls in dance recitals give sexually charged performances dressed in burlesque fashion, yet we clutch our chests in panic at the thought of them walking to school or playing at the park by themselves. It seems we could be less hypervigilant about them falling from the play fort and more obsessed with protecting them from marketers' schemes.

I see childhood as a time for unstructured play fueled by powerful imaginations. As noted educator Maria Montessori said, "Play is the work of the child." Yet when we go toy shopping for our children, we see gendered, sexualized, violent, and nonstimulating one-dimensional toys. Why do our kids seem to respond to these stereotypes?

For an answer I turned to my colleagues from the Sanford Harmony Program, an organization devoted to studying and bridging the gender divide among children. Stacie Foster, project director of the program and a research professor in the T. Denny Sanford School of Social and Family Dynamics at Arizona State University, offered some insight.

> Do the toys you see marketed to kids accurately reflect the people you know in real life? If not, point out to your child that her daddy cooks all the time, your family doctor or mechanic is a woman, and the neighbor lady is a firefighter. ❈

"Part of what makes gendered messages so influential is that children are cognitively primed to absorb them," says Foster. "Children have a natural tendency to sort things—including people—into categories in order to make sense of a complex world. Gender is a particularly salient category because it is visual, concrete, and simple. When children (and adults) consistently encounter messages about gender that go unchallenged, [those messages] naturally contribute to the stereotypes they are forming about gender and about what they as a male or female should be, do, and like."

The good news is parents have the power to challenge and change these stereotypes and to teach their kids to do the same, to their kids' benefit. Foster goes on, "Research has shown that more flexible (rather than rigidly stereotyped) thinking and more diverse interests and preferences are associated with better social and academic outcomes for children." What better way to encourage flexible, diverse interests in kids than through flexible, diverse toys?

> Do your child's toys seem inviting to both boys and girls? Do they support both genders playing together? ❋

My feeling is that play should be about choice. If a girl loves all toys pink and frilly, that is wonderful. If a boy loves trucks and pirate ships, that is superfantastic. But let's allow our children to come to those choices on their own and not push colors or a gender-role agenda on them. Our homes should have toys and attitudes that allow boys and girls to play together so they can develop healthy attitudes toward one another. Pink is not the enemy, girly is not the enemy; lack of choice is the enemy.

The Value of Coed and Diverse Play

When adults introduce their gender stereotypes to children, they greatly limit and skew not only how kids see themselves but also how they see kids of the opposite sex. While there are differences in the sexes, as neuroscientist Lise Eliot examines in her book *Pink Brain, Blue Brain: How Small Differences Grow into Troublesome Gaps—and What We Can Do About It*, "Infant brains are so malleable that small differences at birth become amplified over time, as parents, teachers, peers—and the culture at large—unwittingly reinforce gender stereotypes. Children themselves exacerbate the differences by playing to their modest strengths. They constantly exercise those 'ball-throwing' or 'doll-cuddling' circuits, rarely straying from their comfort zones." Eliot posits that if we can "appreciate how sex differences emerge—rather than assuming them to be fixed biological facts—we can help all children reach their fullest potential, close the troubling gaps between boys and girls, and ultimately end the gender wars that currently divide us."

The researchers from the Sanford Harmony Program stress the need for boys and girls to be able to play together. Among the many benefits of doing so for both sexes are several that help boys to see girls in a more positive way. SHP notes that playing together "increases kids' comfort and familiarity with each other" and "aids in disproving stereotypes."

Most young children of preschool age know three hard facts about themselves: their name, their age, and whether they are a boy or a girl. Because kids' brains are so malleable at this age, this is a key time to teach them there are many ways to be a girl and many ways to be a boy. The cultural gap between boys and girls is troubling. As parents we need to find ways to close the gap by offering our children fewer gendered toys and more ideas for free play and outside play. Boys and girls need opportunities to play together, alongside one another, and in friendly competition.

I have worked diligently to keep our home gender equal, with toys and play spaces full of playthings that allow for open-ended play and lots of imagination. We try to provide toys that foster creativity and

> "When children are consistently encouraged to recognize variability, they are better able to explore their interests and preferences outside of the confines of stereotypes and avoid making rigid assumptions about others."—Sanford Harmony Program ❋

> Plasticity is the idea in neuroscience that a child's brain can be molded and changed by experience—all the more reason to assert there is no such thing as "girl toys" and "boy toys." Let's look at them as "brain toys." ❋

curiosity. All are primary colored or have gender-neutral tones that indicate to the little friends who come to play at our home that all toys are for everyone.

Each child has his or her own toys that are special just to him or her, but that is based more on particular interests than gender. Raising both a boy and a girl, I see their fascination with various topics run all over the place. My daughter has been obsessed with whales and giant squid for a couple of years now, which was a nice change of pace from tarantulas, her obsession during her third year of life. My son loves to build houses out of wooden blocks that his plastic dinosaurs live in. A Baryonyx serves as the mother dinosaur that teaches the rest of the herd in school.

It is understandable that with everything down to babies' teething rings being color-coded by gender, parents might feel like there is no way to keep stereotypes out of their homes. It can be a long, hard search to find an item that isn't color-coded or character-branded. There is also the seemingly unavoidable princess culture beckoning to your daughter.

Below are some toy-related guidelines my husband and I followed when our daughter was a baby and toddler (before she could voice her own opinions and preferences for certain products):

❋ We tried to keep character-branded items out of the house for as long as possible. These are usually clearly directed at one gender or the other.

❋ The toys and items we did purchase had to fit our "skittles rule"—they represented a rainbow of colors. This rule is super-fun to apply while at IKEA.

❋ We focused on her development stages when buying toys. Her gender was never a factor in this. When she was learning to crawl, we got tennis balls and chunky toy cars that would encourage her to move around as she played. When she was learning to stand and walk, she had a toy kitchen, grill, play garden, and tool bench to encourage her to stand while playing and strengthen her leg muscles and improve her balance.

✸ We watched very little television until age two, when she began to watch *Sesame Street*, *The Wonder Pets*, and *Dora the Explorer*, which have nice ensemble casts of male and female characters working together.

When Amelia entered her preschool years, we adjusted our strategies somewhat:

✸ We still limited what came into our home but accepted we had less control over what she encountered outside of it. For example, I didn't freak out when the school nurse would automatically reach for princess stickers instead of the dinosaur ones, or if Amelia played with Barbies during a playdate.

✸ We continued to attempt to keep character-branded items out of the house, but at age three she fell hard for Dora.

✸ We intentionally did not introduce her to the Disney princesses, but she seemed more inclined toward dinosaurs, art, and block building anyway. Around age four she became ravenous for puzzles and painting.

✸ When we did go toy shopping we did so either online for specific items or by browsing at the independent learning toy store in town, not one of the big box shops.

✸ By this age she was developing fine motor skills, so playing with Play-Doh and doing art projects were daily events.

✸ We held playdates at parks in nice weather or took seasonal trips to the apple orchard, zoo, or pumpkin patch. When we were at a playdate where we were guests, Amelia was allowed to play with whatever belonged to the host child.

✸ Dress-up clothes allowed her to role-play, so we had doctor, firefighter, chef, and scientist gear along with fancy dresses, tutus, and all kinds of pants, hats, and shirts in a variety of colors. We used hand-me-down flower girl dresses for princess dresses instead of the $50 options from the Disney Store.

✸ We went to the library one to two times per week and found books that mirrored her current interests. When she was nuts for dinosaurs at age three, my husband created characters for all of her plastic dinos. They became known as "Leroy the Jive-Talking Dinosaur and his Friends." It was hilarious to listen to them play, but this also got her interested in checking out books on volcanoes, the Ice Age, quicksand, prehistoric oceans, and paleontology. When she went crazy for Dora, we checked out books on monkeys, Central American countries and culture, the rain forest, and *National Geographic* explorers.

❊ At this age she also loved dance parties, parades with her toy instruments, building with blocks, making blanket forts, putting on puppet shows, teaching her baby brother how to use toys, and exploring outside.

Now that Amelia is through her preschool years and into her elementary school years, she obviously has a lot of influences from friends. She attends public school and is not sheltered from anything, but her playmates are from families whose values align with our own. Some elementary strategies and experiences:

❊ The vast majority of her screen media is about girls and nature: *Nim's Island, Free Willy 4, Judy Moody and the Not Bummer Summer, Ramona and Beezus, Finding Nemo, Rio, Dolphin Tale, The Land Before Time, Charlotte's Web, Nanny McPhee, Aquamarine, Brave,* and countless educational videos about the ocean have been favorites.

❊ She has great playdates with her pals and transitions well from playing princesses one minute to trying to catch catfish with their bare hands (or face) the next.

❊ Her playtime with pals now largely includes imaginary story lines they act out, usually with a great amount of noise. She also enjoys role-play scenarios, such as restaurant or science lab.

❊ Dress up is still popular, as is fort building (inside and outside).

❊ When she needs quiet time or downtime after school, books, drawing, and educational games for her Leapster Explorer keep her brain chugging but let her body rest.

❄ Art projects are more popular than ever. During playdates I'll help the kids with large-scale projects, like going crazy with a roll of butcher paper and finger paints outside on the patio. Early education blogs and Pinterest are great resources for project ideas.

As girls move into upper elementary school and middle school, time spent with peers shifts from play to hanging out. This time together is still important as they discuss experiences, share secrets and ambitions, and act silly together to blow off steam from the pressures of becoming more grown up every day. Some tips for having your home be a welcome, girl-positive hangout at this age are:

❄ Have healthy foods on hand, such as ingredients for smoothies or a fruit and cheese plate, while your daughter and her friends work on homework together.

❄ Allow for responsible use of technology such as making silly videos of one another on their tablet, Skyping with an out-of-state friend, Instagramming pictures of a fashion show, or using a karaoke app. Be very clear about what is and isn't appropriate use of technology in your home, and the consequences for falling short of expectations.

❄ Be willing to host movie nights or yard games (capture the flag, kick the can, ghost in the graveyard), with lots of popcorn and Italian sodas on hand. Your house might become a zoo, but you've given the kids a safe and supervised place to hang out.

❄ This is a great age for a couple of friends to start a small business together, such as dog walking, yard work, or babysitting. They can learn responsibility and money-management skills while having fun with one another.

❄ Sports are critical at this age for positive peer involvement and positive body image. Have the girls walk down to the soccer field or basketball courts and meet them there with a snack in an hour. Better yet, show up with their moms and challenge them to a game! If team sports aren't her thing, try hiking, biking, or dance.

❋ Girls this age can also gain a lot from volunteer opportunities such as helping with a community theater group, assisting with religious education, working at an animal shelter, or being a candy striper at the hospital.

Broken down by age, here is a list of toys that I believe all kids should have access to as they grow. The small businesses we shop from are listed in the Resources section at the end of the book. I am not a fan of battery-operated toys, especially for little ones, so assume that these suggestions are for battery-free toys. You have the option to buy toys new, but remember that rummage sales, hand-me-downs, Craigslist, and freecycle sites can be your best friend. And remember the Skittles rule: a rainbow of color!

> *Toys should be powered by imagination, not batteries. Allow your child to make her own sound effects and manipulate the toys on her own.* ❋

Birth–age 2

❋ Brightly colored baby toys that encourage manipulations like shaking, rattling, twisting, lifting flaps, feeling textures

❋ Soft dolls or stuffed animals

❋ Balls—bouncy playground balls, hard plastic with toys inside (Fisher-Price Roll-a-Rounds)

❋ Shape sorters and baby puzzles (4 to 6 pieces)

❋ Nesting toys

❋ Wooden blocks

❋ Chunky crayons and finger paints (shaving cream works too)

❋ Musical toys (including pots, pans, and wooden spoons)

❋ Water play in the tub or baby pool, sand toys

❋ Play household items: phone, vacuum cleaner, lawn mower, shopping cart

Ages 3–5

- ❄ Interlocking building blocks such as Duplos (LEGOs usually work well for kids 4½ years and up)
- ❄ More advanced puzzles (12 to 48 pieces)
- ❄ Art supplies, art supplies, and more art supplies
- ❄ Coloring supplies and drawing paper of different sizes and colors
- ❄ Role-play items such as a kitchen set, doctor kits, a cash register, and play food
- ❄ Dress-up clothes for careers, fairy wings, tutus, fancy dress, hats, wizard robe, superhero cape and mask (check with friends for old Halloween costumes)
- ❄ Gardening tools and a sandbox
- ❄ Stuffed, wooden, or plastic animals: zoo, farm, ocean, safari, jungle, desert, dinosaurs
- ❄ Hand and finger puppets
- ❄ A play tent or blankets to make forts
- ❄ Beginner sport equipment (batting tee and ball, size-3 soccer ball, balance bike)
- ❄ Dolls or stuffed animals, blankets to wrap them in, bottle or special spoon to feed them, toy crib, stroller
- ❄ Beginner science kits
- ❄ Play-Doh or molding clay
- ❄ Sidewalk chalk, bubbles, bouncy balls
- ❄ Toy cars and garage or play mat and/or wooden train set and tracks
- ❄ Dollhouse with family figures
- ❄ Play scenes: airport, farm, zoo, city (Playmobil offers fantastic play sets with equal representation of male and female figures)
- ❄ Easy board games such as Memory or Candy Land and easy card games such as Go Fish
- ❄ Musical instruments
- ❄ Lacing sets

Ages 6–9

- ❄ Add from the list above, but grow your child's specific interests. If your child loves fairies, build a fairy house in the yard. If your child loves zoo animals, create a giant habitat out of cardboard boxes and art supplies.

❁ LEGO (we prefer the giant bags of random bricks; we don't usually buy the kits)

❁ Dolls (American Girl, Journey Girl, and Our Generation dolls offer girls healthy doll play with backstories of travel and American history)

❁ Lalaloopsy (cute and funky dolls that come with pets and show girls and boys being friends together)

❁ Action figures like Spider Man, Wonder Woman, or Bindi Irwin

❁ Great toys for nature lovers from the Animal Planet store and Backyard Safari Outfitters

❁ Dress-up outfits for knights, pirates, mermaids, wizards, mad scientists, and global explorers

❁ Paper dolls

❁ Magic sets

❁ Sports equipment and time for practicing beginner skills outside

❁ More complex science and art projects, puzzles, and board games

❁ More complex construction kits (K'nex, Connectagons, Rokenbok, GoldieBlox, Roominate)

❁ Subscription to a magazine such as *Highlights*, *Puzzlemania*, *Muse*, *Ask*, *Calliope*, or *New Moon Girls*

Ages 10–12

❁ American Girl dolls and their books about girls' place in American history

❁ LEGO Architecture or Creator series or robotics kits

❁ Games such as Skip-Bo, Life, Scrabble, Acuity, Uno, Clue, Skylanders (for the Nintendo Wii)

❁ Complex art and craft projects (focus on a specific skill like throwing pottery or dollmaking or jewelry making, or sign up for an art class together)

❁ Musical instruments like guitar, drums, violin, piano

❁ Perplexus 3-D puzzles

- Complex electric circuit or science experiments (or try your hand at living experiments such as building a terrarium)
- Membership to an art or science museum that offers classes for kids
- Camera and videography equipment so she can tell her own stories
- Blank sketchbooks or journals and an endless supply of pencils

Letters from the Experts
Susan Linn

Susan Linn is the director of the Campaign for a Commercial-Free Childhood (www.commercialfreechildhood.org), an instructor in psychiatry at Harvard Medical School, and the author of *The Case for Make Believe: Saving Play in a Commercialized World* and *Consuming Kids: The Hostile Takeover of Childhood*.

Dear Parents,

Neil Postman, the brilliant author and cultural commentator, once observed, "If parents wish to preserve childhood for their own children, they must conceive of parenting as an act of rebellion against culture." Postman was writing at the dawn of the twenty-first century—as marketing to children was intensifying on television, video games, DVDs, and the Internet—but before the explosion of miniaturized media in the form of cell phones, mp3 players, and tablets. Today it's harder than ever to keep commercial culture at bay.

For parents, rebelling against the culture—or reclaiming childhood from corporate marketers—means acting on two levels. We need to think about other people's children as well as our own. If we are outraged at how girls and women are portrayed in the media, then we need to join forces; many voices are stronger than one voice. Support organizations and advocacy groups that take a public stand against the sexualization of little girls, that hold corporations accountable for foisting egregious sexualized products and marketing on children, and that advocate for policies limiting commercial access to children.

Ensuring that our children have plenty of opportunities for active and creative play is another form of cultural rebellion. For the first time ever, parents have to consciously carve out commercial-free time and space for kids. Around the world, the most common leisure time activity for children is watching television (and the new technologies do not replace TV time, they add to it). For your own kids, make sure there's time to play outdoors. Dirt, sand, water, and mud can occupy children for hours. And remember that the best toys for children are not usually the best-selling toys. The toys that truly encourage creative play are markedly lacking in electronic bells and whistles. They just lay there until a child transforms them into something and can be used repeatedly and in multiple ways.

Stock up on art supplies: crayons, paints, markers, glitter, and glue. Hunt for blocks, dolls, cars, and toy figures that aren't linked to any media program. Fill your house with books and music. Celebrate National Screen-Free Week (www.screen free.org). Remember that it's OK to say no sometimes—especially if you're feeling pressure to buy things that violate your core values and are contrary to what you know is best for your kids.

We pass our values on to our children through the stories we tell them and the toys we give them. The corporate stories driving our commercialized culture aren't good for kids.

The marketplace values of impulse buying, unthinking brand loyalty, belief in the quick fix, me-firstism, greed, and rigid sexualized images of what it means to be male or female are great for promoting consumption essential to corporate profits. But they undermine health and well-being, as well as the essentials of a meaningful life—creativity, cooperation, altruism, and community.

All the best to you and your children,
Susan Linn

To Princess or Not to Princess?

Perhaps noticeably missing from the above lists are an abundance of princesses, tiaras, ball gowns, princess shoes, and fashion dolls. I think princess and fashion play can be a great part of childhood and don't need to be discouraged in a little girl. Girls who love fancy dresses and tea parties and dancing around their pretend castle are wonderful and should be respected and celebrated. Princesses, when left to the imagination of little girls, can be brave and wise and lead great adventures.

But that is generally not how princesses are marketed. Even Merida, our brave and outspoken archer princess, was reduced by the Disney Store and Mattel into a makeup- and ball gown–wearing, pink-and-

> Pink is just a color. Playing princess is just a story line. "Pink culture," also called "princess culture," is vastly different and sends limiting messages to our girls. ❊

purple bow-toting, sparkling magic wand–carrying fairytale. A far cry from the rowdy Scottish lass we saw and loved in the movie *Brave*. Somewhere Brenda Chapman is rolling her eyes (and hopefully writing another girl power screenplay).

The princess bug never bit in our home, partly due to my design, partly due to my daughter's personality. At eight years old, she is now into fairies and mermaids, although we are trying to give her examples other than the Disney varieties. A simple trip to our local children's library and some helpful librarians are all we need to find other stories to learn from and base play on.

Jennifer Hartstein dedicated her 2012 book *Princess Recovery: A How-To Guide to Raising Strong, Empowered Girls Who Can Create Their Own Happily Ever Afters* to "all of the heroines out there . . . enjoy wearing your crown as you play in the mud." Her book serves as an excellent guide for parents to establish balance in their daughters' lives for playing princess and a whole mix of other things. Princess play can be OK, but when it goes overboard, our girls can be missing out on some very valuable life lessons. The jump overboard happens when princess culture consumes a girl, a pattern described by Hartstein as starting off with innocent sparkly dresses like the princesses she sees in the movies; then moving into the trendiest, most scantily clad doll because princesses are now for babies; next comes the makeup and teen fashion styles she sees on young teen pop stars and in the girls section in department stores.

The problem with princess culture is that all of this happens by age ten or so, leaving girlhood to become a mess of age compression and focus on outward appearance and materialism. As Peggy Orenstein says in *Cinderella Ate My Daughter: Dispatches from the Front Lines of the New Girlie-Girl Culture,*

> If your daughter is a "princess girl," attracted to all things royal and sparkly, try to give her an empowered sense of being a princess, something that goes beyond being pretty. Try greeting her as your "brave princess" or "adventurous princess" or "wise princess." Ask her what clever thoughts are swirling under her tiara today or what kind of exploring she is going to do in her fancy dress. ❋

"The innocence of pink signaled during the Princess years, which seem to be so benign, even protective, has receded, leaving behind narcissism and materialism as the hallmarks of feminine identity."

Big Hair and Short Skirts—the "Fashion Doll" Parade

There is no toy on the market that better embodies "narcissism and materialism" than fashion dolls. They are popular toys, brands like Monster High and Barbie (Mattel) or Bratz and Novi Stars (MGA), earning their makers millions in profits. They are also so hypersexualized that I feel they have no place in the homes of young children. I hear from many parents that when their daughters play with the newer Barbie dolls, the clothes are so tightly fit on the doll that the girl can't experiment with fashion and clothing because she can't get her half-naked Barbie undressed. What is the point of having a Barbie if you can't change her clothes? The focus of these dolls, often spelled out in the character's bio conceived by the manufacturer, is beauty, shopping, and fashion. Sometimes they get imaginative and add something about dating boys or wishing to become a pop star. Giggle!

As Lyn Mikel Brown and Sharon Lamb write in *Packaging Girlhood*, what makes these fashion dolls appealing to girls is their ticket into a lavish lifestyle. Brown and Lamb credit Barbie for starting all this, but the Bratz line takes it to a new level. They write, "It's not only the frenzy of consumerism but also the lifestyle itself. Barbie had a dream house to come home to, but her nightlife was ours to create. Bratz gives the dolls a variety of scenes to choose from and tells us how the girls experience them. These are the girls who 'know how important it is to be seen!'" Brown and Lamb liken it to little girls practicing to be sex objects.

That is not the definition of being female that I want for my daughter. I think fashion is great, but it isn't what encompasses me as a woman. I also think a line of realistic, nonsexualized dolls that show women with body diversity and authentic ethnic diversity working in politics, business, medicine and science, technology, and education would be even better.

Some of the toy companies have tried to do a workaround by making dolls with a career theme. If you are going to make career dolls, make them capable of doing the career they represent. The Barbie "I'm a Vet!" doll has a miniskirt and open-toed, high-heeled shoes. It is more *Melrose Place* Pet Vet Barbie than, say, Jane Goodall Barbie. I've seen my vet get into some compromising positions while trying to care for my dogs, and I can't imagine him doing the same in a miniskirt and peekaboo heels.

To be fair, the Barbie "I Can Be" a Nurse and Paleontologist and Teacher dolls didn't make my head explode. Barbie "I Can Be" President is wearing a smart pencil skirt and blazer, and comes in Caucasion, Black, Hispanic, and Asian versions. Amelia often watches *Meet the Press* with me on Sunday mornings, and I could see myself buying her a President Barbie. Amelia owns a Surfer Barbie and Sea World Barbie, which I actually like except for her Cirque de Soleil makeup. We also like the Mermaid Barbie line, because, as mermaids go, they are pretty mystical and dreamlike. So there are some Barbie dolls out there I would consider buying for my daughter, sort of, and if I did I would just shore myself up for some fun body image talks to recalibrate after an hour of playing with Barbie's humanly impossible physical features. Having Barbie dolls that are water-based helps because then she only plays with them when she is in the bathtub. Amelia didn't really begin to play with these until she was well past her sixth birthday, so she had a foundation of critical thinking already in place and will talk to me about body image topics while she plays with her Barbies. She is able to question and challenge the media she is involved with, and that makes me feel like I've won a battle in the war against the marketers for her girlhood and sense of self.

Barbie aside, if we can be frank for a minute, the vast majority of these fashion dolls are about sex. The big hair, heavy makeup, skin-tight pants, booty shorts, micro-miniskirts, lace-up bustiers, fishnets, kneesocks in heels or thigh-high stiletto boots: all of the clothing commonly found on these dolls is also commonly found on sex workers and has been fetishized in pornography.

The newest trend shows dolls with giant hair, enormous and innocent-looking eyes, firm breasts, bared tummies, and the "schoolgirl skirt plus bare upper thigh" combo. Some of this look is influenced by American porn, some by Japanese anime, but let's not split hairs. It ought to give parents pause. Yet it doesn't, and oftentimes I hear these dolls defended by parents. But the fact remains that these dolls are heavily sexualized and require a lot of media literacy interference from parents if they are going to be in the home. Girls are drawn to them because they have the allure of being grown-up and glamorous, but that is because your seven-year-old doesn't understand the difference between haute couture and hooker attire. Parents do understand this difference and need to be more responsible. The companies that make these dolls cover their bottom line on the backs of little girls whom they sexualize with their products.

> Say your girl already owns several fashion dolls, and you are not a fan. Challenge her to expand the story line beyond shopping and clubbing. Can Barbie run a safari camp or be the head organizer for the Paralympics? Maybe the princess dolls can run a school for girls in the hills of Nepal or a sanctuary for a rare species of bear found only in Montana? Can you help your daughter build a mini organic farm for Barbie in the backyard? Anything is possible with a little imagination! ❋

Is that really the best we can do for our daughters? And what is this teaching our sons about girls and women? And why is this selling so well? When did twelve inches of plastic sparkly sex become OK for our kids to play with? And where, for the love of Goddess, is a Maya Angelou or Queen Elizabeth I or Joan of Arc doll in this melee of sexualized and exploited femininity?

"It's Just a Doll"? Thinking Critically and Thinking Twice

At some point, your daughter will beg you for some form of sexualized doll because they are everywhere and because many of her classmates will have them. Or someone will get her one as a gift. What to do?

I'll tell you about my experiences with my girl and about what's worked for other Pigtail Pals parents. This is an ongoing conversation, the depth of which changes as she matures. And it is an imperfect conversation, because so many times what really needs to be said can't be said to a child. It can be extremely difficult to explain to your girl why you object to the dolls when she's at an age when you don't want to introduce topics like prostitution and eating disorders.

In talking to my daughter, I have tried to focus not on criticizing her for liking these dolls but rather on critiquing the way they are made, and on working with her to compare that to our family values and the people we love and respect. I also make sure not to criticize other girls who like or play with these dolls.

Whether you are in the toy aisle faced with a pleading child or want to talk to her about a gift she already received, try some of these probing yet gentle prompts and responses to get her thinking critically about and maybe even challenging this unhealthy media:

"Those dolls look a little too grown-up for us."

"I don't like the messages those dolls give; they don't feel healthy to me."

"That doll is dressed so much like a grown-up, I think it is meant for much older girls."

"That doll dresses too grown-up for her age, so she needs to stay here until her mommy can change her clothes." (A good one for those under age four.)

"I think that doll might have a hard time doing fun things in those sorts of clothes, do you? It might be hard to run and jump and really use her body. In our family we know bodies are for being active and having adventures, so let's find a doll that can do all the great things you like to do."

"The doll is wearing clothing that wouldn't be practical for heroic adventures, and she would have to stay home til she changed."

"Why do you want that doll?" or "What do you like about that doll?" (Listen to the answers.)

"Hmmm. Why do you think she's dressed like that? What do you think she is going to do? Could you wear that to school/soccer/shopping/play?"

"Are there any dolls here that look like you? Are they wearing clothing that you could wear to school/to play soccer /to run at the park? I think those dolls would be a better fit for our family."

Below are some more detailed conversations and responses that have taken place in our house that might help you find the right words in yours.

Barbie High and Pointy

"Hey, Mom, why are Barbie's feet high and pointy?"

"Because she always wears high heels."

"Yeah, but she is supposed to be a surfer, so how can she surf in heels?"

"I know, right? Doesn't make much sense to me. Maybe she leaves her heels on the beach."

"And a shark *eats* her! Rawrrrerrr!!" offers Benny, Amelia's little brother. Ben and I fist-bump.

"Ugh, Ben. And Mom? Why does she wear so much makeup? Bindi doesn't wear makeup but she also surfs and she has the right kind of feet. Her makeup would wash off . . ." Amelia trails off. I can tell she is sorting it out in her head, so I let it marinate for a few moments.

"Yes, I suppose it would. I don't wear makeup when I swim because it seems silly and it would wash off."

"Mom, you wear makeup so you don't look so tired. Maybe that is why Barbie wears it."

"Darling, Barbie does not have children. I don't think she is as tired as Mommy is. I think she just always wears makeup."

"Mom, why are her legs longer than Bindi's legs?"

"Well, Barbie is supposed to be an adult, and Bindi is a kid, so Barbie is taller. Barbie is like, twenty-five, and Bindi is only twelve. But if Barbie were a real-life person, her body could not look like that. Her body wouldn't function the way it needs to in order to be healthy."

"Huh," says Amelia.

"Huh," says I.

Meanie Monsters

Ever seen a Monster High doll? They look like they could rip your head off and stomp on it with their platform heels. When the subject first came up with my daughter, I made clear to her that they were dressed in a way that I felt was inappropriate for children, that their faces looked mean, not nice, and that their bodies sent our hearts unhealthy messages. We talked about different colors of hair and skin being really cool, but that these dolls made little girls focus too much on being pretty for other people and being too grown-up, and that is not what kids need to do.

A few months down the road, when the dolls came up again, I told her that they have the kind of bodies that can make girls sick, because a real person could never have a body like that, and that I loved my little girl's healthy body so much I would never want her to have something that would make her think her body wasn't amazing. We talked about impossibly long and thin legs, teeny tiny torsos, and giant heads and took measurements of our own body ratios to compare.

And when she kept pushing the issue by talking about the clothing being cool, I told her that girls who dress like that often don't have full and happy hearts, and they use clothing like that to get attention and make themselves feel full. We talked about the difference between feeling valuable because other people find you pretty and feeling valuable because you know you are full of awesome. (I was very careful not to use pejoratives or slut-shame the dolls, but in all honesty "cheap hooker" is what was going through my head.) I told Amelia that she would not be allowed to dress that way when she is a teen and that she might find it hard to earn the respect of her college professors and future employers or employees if she dresses like she is ready to party instead of work hard. This was an imperfect conversation for a perfectly age-inappropriate topic.

Then I took it a step further and we agreed to try a little experiment. We went upstairs to her dress-up drawer and picked out clothes that were much too small and tight for her. She put them on and tried to play but quickly found she couldn't move freely. We then made the connection that maybe Monster High dolls were silly, because how could those girls move around and be teenagers who do fun things and play sports? Amelia said she thought maybe they just stood around and looked pretty.

I hope to grow the idea of "full and happy hearts" as Amelia ages. Do Monster High dolls appear to have full and happy hearts? I don't think anyone could objectively say they do. As Amelia gets older we'll also talk about what it means to have a "personal brand" and how we represent ourselves to others in the community and earn their respect. I hope these things help her make good and healthy decisions about all kinds of things: diet and exercise, drugs and alcohol, sex and relationships, good behavior in school, and so on. If this is our baseline, I believe she will see the things that fall so far outside of that—whether it is Monster High or music lyrics and videos or friends who are a bad influence—for what they are and be that much more equipped to make good choices for herself.

La Dee Da, Bratz, Bratzillaz, Winx Club, and the Next Noxious Brand to Come Along

While watching TV together one morning Amelia and I had this conversation:

"Mom, are La Dee Da dolls appropriate? I don't think they have too much makeup on." "Well, some of their outfits are really creative, and their hair is supercool. But some of their skirts are really short, and they are wearing other items that are usually just for grown-ups, like fishnet stockings and high heels."

"Well, I think they wear high heels because they live in the city," suggests Amelia.

"Oh, maybe. Except the dolls are supposedly sixteen. Auntie Courtney and Auntie Lisa and Louise and Lindsey live in big cities. Do they wear high heels and makeup like that?"

"Well, Auntie Lisa can't because it isn't safe to wear heels in Africa. I think Auntie Courtney and Louise do when they go out for nights of fashion."

"Oh, right," I say. "Auntie Courtney does have some fancy heels she wears for special occasions. The only time Auntie Courtney and I have worn makeup like that was in high school when we were being silly for homecoming."

"Well, Lindsey can't wear heels in her science lab because if she drops a beaker of chemicals, her toes will melt off and she'll become a zombie."

"Totally. I think their bodies look like sticks with big heads on top. They look like lollipops."

"Yeah, they do look like lollipops. So, can I get one of these? They just don't make nice dolls these days."

"You got that right, sister. Amelia, I want you to realize these dolls aren't too bad compared to some others, but all they are about is fashion. These dolls are just about *wearing* fashion and looking pretty. I'd like it better if they were students at a design school in New York City and this into fashion. But when wearing cute clothes is their only attribute . . . I just want you to realize the four women we talked about who we know in real life all have great wardrobes, but they are also a photographer in Africa, a vice president at a communications firm, a researcher for the government, and a PhD student in chemistry. They all have traveled the world, gone to college, gone to graduate school, and two of them have babies. I'm just saying, there is more to life than fancy eye makeup and supercute dresses."

"I know, Mom. There's also zombie experiments. What if when I play with these dolls, I will pretend they are going to college to be president?"

"President of what, Smalls?"

"The United States."

Ultimately, parents can be responsible consumers. This trend in trashy dolls is not going away any time soon; it is unfortunately making manufacturers way too much money. Mattel's hypersexualized mean girl Monster High brand earned them profits in the millions of dollars during the second quarter of 2012. In 2008 Mattel sued MGA for copyright infringement over the Bratz line. Because if there is one legacy a business for children wants to leave behind, it is 100 percent market share of foot-tall oversexed dolls for grade-school divas.

The market will carry what it can bear, and as long as there is an audience and a consumer for it, companies will continue to make it. We'll talk more in chapter 10 about how to use your voice with retailers and manufacturers, and I list positive toy companies you can support in the Resources guide.

Tech Toys

Parents today are navigating the uncharted waters of the Internet and other technology "toys" of choice for tweens and even younger girls. Technology can be a blessing, of course, but unfortunately it has also opened up brand-new avenues for sexualizing girls to much larger populations.

I am eternally grateful that texting, Tumblr, and Facebook were not around when I was a teen. I needed space to unplug from my peers and social life, focus on my studies, and, frankly, focus on myself. I'm glad that my youthful indiscretions are not captured for eternity on a social media site. Technology is everywhere and it is powerful, so how do we harness that power into positive and productive experiences for our girls?

★ Assess whether your child demonstrates the maturity required for social media: speaking respectfully to others (even when disagreeing), recognizing cyberbullying and not engaging in it, recognizing anything she says can be made public at any time, understanding the importance of age-appropriate content (hardcore porn and "thinspiration"—communities revolving

around photo-sharing apps that encourage eating disorders—
are ubiquitous online, are you ready to have those conversations?), and recognizing the importance of time and sleep
management.

✺ Set up a policy for family expectations of "digital citizenship"
and the consequences if those policies are not followed. Part
of that policy must include password access to her accounts
and the right to check in on her activity at any time (this also
includes texts and pictures on her phone). Another part of that
policy is that at no time is she to send pictures or video of body
parts to someone or reveal personal information to strangers
(and help her define "strangers," because the Internet blurs that
concept for kids).

✺ Talk about content value—such as song lyrics or jokes from TV
or a movie she streamed that may go against the personal brand
you are helping her build.

✺ Show her how to safely explore the world through her device,
like using Face Time with a friend's cousin in another country to practice a foreign language or listening to TEDx talks
(http://tedxtalks.ted.com) on girl empowerment, media literacy, and positive body image. Help her create Pinterest boards
of places she wants to go, books she wants to read, inspiration
for photographs she wants to take, objects or people she wants
to paint, and things she wants to build or cook.

✺ Reserve the right to review her downloaded content. I don't
necessarily advocate banning music you do not approve of, but
I do suggest having conversations around the meaning of lyrics
or lifestyles promoted by the artists she listens to. For example,
I loved Jefferson Airplane and the Rolling Stones when I was in
high school, but I never wanted to do drugs or get high. I just
liked the music, and my mom helped me decode the meanings
behind the songs.

✺ Be aware there is an endless supply of apps and programs for
kids which instantly delete texts or redirect parental control

software. It can be difficult to stay ahead of all of it, and you have no control over it. But you do have influence over your child, so really focus on instilling digital-citizenship values in her that help her make the right decisions, because playing "cop" to all her online use will leave you exhausted.

❊ Set limits such as no cell phones at the dinner table or family movie night (and make sure you follow them as well!); set daily time limits for social media use, and insist devices charge in the parents' room overnight. An idea I learned at the Campaign for a Commercial-Free Childhood media literacy summit is taking a family "Digital Sabbath" and turning all technology off for a twenty-four-hour period.

My hope is parents start to (or continue to) look more critically at the toys and products they allow in the home, and recognize the influence they have on children. We teach "please and thank you" long before our kids understand manners, and many families teach bedtime prayers long before kids understand religion. We do this because we want to lay a foundation for the people we hope for them to become. And so it is with toys and the importance they play in childhood: let's provide our daughters with toys that reinforce the messages we are teaching them about the women we wish them to grow up to be.

Our kids are soaking in every bit of information they can from the environment we provide. We should ensure they are feasting on media that leave their hearts and brains empowered, happy, and healthy.

Letters from the Experts

Melanie Klein

Melanie Klein is an associate faculty member in the department of sociology and women's studies at Santa Monica College.

Dear Parent,

I'm a child of the seventies, a decade marked by the countercultural movement that rocked the stifling conventions of mainstream society; *Free to Be . . . You and Me* (the gender-liberating album by Marlo Thomas and friends); the launch of *Ms.* magazine; and marked by a rainbow of possibility for all boys and girls.

My girlhood wasn't awash in a sea of Pepto-Bismol pink or cleavage-baring princesses. In fact, the Little Golden Books I read featured *Peter Pan*'s baby Michael and *Lady and the Tramp*'s new "baby human" in pink onesies. *The Wizard of Oz*'s Dorothy, *Pinocchio*'s "Blue Fairy," and *Peter Pan*'s Wendy wore various shades of light blue. My early childhood bedroom donned a fairy-tale theme devoid of doe-eyed, pinkified princesses and later on rocked a safari theme. Pink was simply one option from a vast color spectrum. While I certainly adored princesses and fairies (and I owned dozens of Barbies), I also played adventurers while sporting a sword on my hip and coveted my tool set.

My childhood was nothing short of magical, a time filled with creativity and endless possibility. It was marked by wonder and imaginative play. I feel fortunate to have grown up during a time when gender expectations had opened up a bit, when gender constraints weren't laced quite as tight. Don't get me wrong, expectations of what it meant to be a male child or a female child were present. They just didn't seem as ominous as they do today. As opposed to propelling forward on that momentum allowing a full range of expression (ultimately allowing everyone the opportunity to self-actualize in authentic ways), we've regressed as a culture.

In August 2010, a seventeen-month-old boy was beaten to death for "being too girly." The event was disturbing enough in itself, but as the mother of a boy who was the same age at that time, I was haunted and heartbroken. Around the same period, a five-year-old boy was taunted and accused of being gay for choosing to dress up like Daphne from *Scooby-Doo* for Halloween, a boy who liked pink dresses caused headline news, and a high school football player was kicked off the field for wearing pink cleats during Breast Cancer Awareness Month. A J. Crew ad featuring a boy wearing pink toe nail polish and lovingly playing with his mother caused a conservative outcry lambasting his mother for being "irresponsible." The backlash accused J. Crew and the featured parent of celebrating transgendered children and of contributing to "confused" gender identities and creating gendered propaganda.

It's obvious that social expectations regarding what is appropriate and acceptable for boys and girls are becoming increasingly rigid, stifling, and too often dangerous. The reactions and social outcry against those who dare to be themselves reflect the dangerous world of gender policing. I'm committed to expanding opportunities for our children. I'm committed to creating a social environment that supports the limitless imaginations of our boys and girls. And if you've picked up this book, I suspect you agree.

Melanie Klein

Around the Kitchen Table— Fat Talk and Body Image

Everything in this book is really about this chapter. If we are honest about it, our culture values and judges women and girls based on the level of attractiveness of their bodies. It is a time-honored tradition that too few women are rebuking and teaching their daughters to reject as well. It is a tradition that sets women up for failure and inhibits our daughters from loving themselves and taking pride in who they are, as they are. In the age of obesity, eating disorders, omnipresent marketing, Photoshop, and celebrity worship, we parents need to begin to create some new traditions for our daughters that include body confidence, acceptance, a little reality, and healthful messages.

Our culture teaches our girls to be a hot body first and a mind second (or not at all). The definition of what is an acceptable body is often so narrow that it is generally unachievable for most of the population. There is so much emphasis put on being seen as attractive and desirable, usually to the exclusion of all other things, that girls internalize these values, and we are seeing it take an emotional and psychological toll on them. These girls become young women who become mothers, and the cycle continues. The mothers become grandmothers, yet, despite what should be wisdom in years, the cycle continues.

We must break this cycle. The population with the fastest-growing rate of eating disorders, aside from children under twelve years old, is the elderly. From cradle to grave, it would seem, women are conditioned never to love our bodies. Really, is that any way to live? Are we really accepting that half of the population should be unhappy in their skin?

What saddens me the most is how the human body is perpetually distorted rather than celebrated in the media, and we continue to accept that distortion and measure ourselves against it. The media break girls and women down, piece them apart, and turn them into objects to be accepted or rejected. If a young woman falls short, there is surely a product or twenty out there that she can purchase to help her "fix" herself. Hair. Eyes. Lips. Perfectly round, perky breasts. Slender arms. Tiny waist and tight tummy. Simultaneously curvy and narrow hips. Toned thighs, but not too toned. Gym bunny toned, not athlete toned. Perky butt. Sexy calves and ankles. Pedicured toes. Congratulations, it's a girl.

But we didn't give birth to pieces of a girl. We welcomed into our arms a whole human being, perfect in every way, and we made a promise to her to love her, all of her. We need to make a new promise: that as parents we will teach her how to love herself.

Mothers-to-be have written to me concerned about their unborn daughter's body image. Young women who are not even married yet have written, concerned about the body image of the children they may *someday* have with their future spouse. The mother of a two-and-a-half-year-old girl wrote to me to say that one night her toddler was wearing a nightgown, smoothed it over her round belly, stepped on the scale, and said in her baby-like voice that she needed to lose a few pounds. Another mom asked for advice on what to tell her five-year-old after the child grabbed her thighs saying she hated them. My own daughter has told me she wishes I were skinnier, adding "long legs are the prettiest."

There seems to be no end to the body insecurity or outright body hate going on. I hear "fat talk" everywhere I go—at the pet shop when the woman in front of me declined the free candy bar offered because she didn't want to "lose her figure," at the school family fun night when a bunch of moms sat on the side of the pool and made cracks about their bodies and joked about how brave I was to be in a swimsuit in the middle of winter, at the library while I waited for a cup of coffee as two ladies greeted each other by discussing who was thinner, during a get-together with friends when the women trashed on their bodies for being too fat. And my daughter hears all of this, too.

As parents we need to start taking the idea of teaching positive body image seriously, and to start this teaching early—believe it or not, when the child is still in diapers. Poor body image has become a problem for the majority of children by the time they enter kindergarten. What, exactly, is the research telling us?

- ✤ A 2008 Australian study of fifty-three preschoolers revealed many of them had already picked up messages like "fat is bad" and "skinny is healthy." The four-year-old girls showed they have been taught to be weight conscious, while the boys demonstrated the knowledge to "eat more in order to bulk up."
- ✤ Nearly half of three- to six-year-old girls worry about becoming fat.
- ✤ 42 percent of first- to third-grade girls want to be thinner.
- ✤ 81 percent of ten-year-olds are afraid of becoming fat and have admitted to dieting.
- ✤ 53 percent of thirteen-year-old girls are unhappy with their bodies.
- ✤ 78 percent of seventeen-year-old girls are unhappy with their bodies and 32 percent of them admit to starving themselves to lose weight.
- ✤ 65 million American girls and women have reported disordered eating or having an eating disorder.

As a parent, as a woman, these numbers are disheartening. This is a massive societal problem. It feels overwhelming, almost as if there is no starting or ending point. Except there is a point where it all changes. That point is me. That point is you. Envision it like this: Your daughter is a young tree and has several rings that make up her core. As her parent, you are the starting point for your daughter's healthy body image. Your relationship with and the way you speak about your own body and will greatly impact your daughter's views about hers. The next ring out is your responsibility to make sure you are teaching her about healthy body image early on. The next ring includes messages coming from her other parent (and stepparents) and siblings. Next are her home environment and her media, her friends, then her extended family, family friends, then teachers and coaches. Every person in her life becomes a ring, with her at the center and you protectively encircling her, making sure she grows tall and straight and strong.

The number-one gift a mother can give her daughter is a positive self-image in the face of rampant cultural stereotypes and media sexualization. How your daughter feels about herself will impact everything she does, every decision she makes. Dads play a big role too. Whatever your family makeup is, let's decide here and now that with us, it starts to change.

Let's Make Some Changes

Here are some effective general actions we can take no matter our child's age to support positive body image in our daughters, as well as more strategies by age range.

- ❀ Knock off the fat talk. Negative statements about your own or others' bodies (weight, size, food that goes in it) have to stop. This includes talk among guests in your home, and during social settings. Stop vocally giving your daughter permission to hate herself by tearing down your body or the bodies of others.
- ❀ Focus your comments about your daughter's body on what she is doing and accomplishing with her body, not how it looks.

Whether she is taking her first steps or tearing it up in varsity basketball, make your comments count toward building up her sense of self-worth. Hear the difference between "Oh, pretty girl, look at you!" and "There's my big girl using her strong legs! We've got a walker!"

❈ Provide clothes for your daughter that allow her to play and move. I hear from so many teachers and coaches that girls today do not know how to take up space with their bodies or fully use the range of their bodies because they are restricted by tight or revealing clothing, inappropriate footwear, and self-consciousness.

If your daughter is little, realize that most of the young adult apparel is simply age-compressed down into the girls' department; those styles aren't really designed for a growing and playing child's body. Find clothing that is appropriate for the demands of an active childhood. While department stores and big box shops are usually the biggest offenders when it comes to inappropriate girls' clothing, smaller or specialty retailers including Hanna Andersson, L.L.Bean, Lands' End, Carter's, and Crazy 8 routinely offer durable and attractive play clothes.

If your daughter is older, help her make apparel choices that reflect the personal brand you want her to project, meaning: who she is, what she stands for, and how she values herself (more on this in chapter 9). And give her the space to make a bad choice every now and then; it teaches her that she has agency over her body.

❈ Eat healthfully as a family. It is not complicated to teach our kids the value of nutritious foods and the idea of eating less healthy foods only in moderation. We don't want to teach our kids that foods are "good" or "bad" or that eating a particular food makes you "good" or "bad," but at the same time we need to get real about the difference between a fresh peach and a basket of fried mozzarella sticks. Food is a source of fuel and enjoyment in life and should not be turned into a source of shame and anxiety.

❊ Make meals a time of gathering together. The best time to teach your children to have a healthy relationship with food is during family meals. A lot of us have lost this tradition, with hectic work and activity schedules, but family mealtime is important. The idea of coming together for meals is as old as time, and there is a reason for it. It allows us to be grateful for the food in front of us and what it means in our life. It allows us to slow down, connect, and communicate. A family meal, once a day or at least a few times a week, allows us to show our children that food nourishes us physically, while the people we love nourish us emotionally.

❊ Let your daughter see and hear you enjoying life with your awesome body. Take family walks or bike rides, go play catch outside or do yoga on the patio, walk like a queen/king in your bathing suit. By showing your daughter that our bodies are instruments, not ornaments, life takes on a different meaning. An ornament is meant to be gazed at and set up high to be admired for its prettiness. An instrument has the purpose of creating and doing. If I had been preoccupied with what I looked like while bungee jumping off a crane in Amsterdam, scuba diving in the French Riviera, horseback riding in Mexico, diving into waterfalls in Hawaii, or exploring caves in South Africa, I might not have done any of those things. I didn't want to wait for that "perfect body" before I did all these amazing things; I wanted to live my life. When we stop caring so much about what our bodies look like, we are completely free to enjoy all of the things our bodies can do.

After spending several years talking with thousands of parents on social media and in workshops, I have come away with the feeling that we do actually know that teaching our daughters to love their bodies is best for them, but our own insecurities and hang-ups get in the way. We need to first reject what the media tells us about our looks and define beauty for ourselves. *We* decide what beautiful means, and we are really missing out if we wake up each day feeling like anything less.

Let's commit to getting out of our own way, stopping our own body hate, and passing on new traditions of body love and acceptance to our daughters.

Body Image Begins in Diapers

You can begin to shape your daughter's body image before she is able to walk and talk. I think it is important for a girl to be told all through her childhood and in a meaningful way that she is "pretty" or "beautiful," if families can deepen the definition of those words to go beyond the exterior to become a feeling and a way of being. Taking pride in how you look as an individual is a powerful thing, and nothing looks better than confidence and charisma. You can balance those compliments with messages that her body is strong, capable, and trustworthy. What better time to do that than while she is an infant, exploring all her amazing parts? I'm sure you've seen a baby lose herself in delight over discovering her knees, or that she can slap her hand on the bare floor with a terrific noise, or bounce while tightly gripping the edge of the couch on those deliciously chubby baby thighs.

Here are some ways I shared this with Amelia when she was a baby:

* ✻ During baths, I would name each part that I was washing and what it allowed her body to do. This continued as she grew, and as a toddler she loved playing the "name game" and showing me all of her different body parts.
* ✻ Amelia started rolling over and scooching around three to four months, and full-on crawling right at six months. My husband and I would lie on our bellies just a few feet away from her and tell her she was our big, strong girl. We would encourage her to use her strong muscles and come get us. Having her parents' faces and outstretched arms right there was a big motivator, and she would kick and giggle and drool her way over to us. Sometimes she would tip over and get stuck on her back. We cheered her on to right herself and try again. She was learning

the strength and dependability of her body, and we were learning to let her solve her own problems and allow her control over her body (instead of reaching in to save her).

❈ We made feeding times a calm family event. When she was tiny, breast/bottle feedings were a chance for bonding (and the other parent to shower). When she was a bigger baby, table feedings were about trying new foods and textures, enjoying food, and relating food to nourishment. We would say things like, "Who's going to grow so big and strong today with these nums?" (*Nums* was Amelia's word for all food) or "Does that tummy feel good with healthy food in it?" We taught Amelia baby sign language so that she could tell us when she wanted more, or when she was full. We respected her when she told us she hated a food (the Green Beans Incident of 2006) and we ate our meals with her so that she saw her family enjoying food. She was allowed to "explore" with her food, usually involving a great mess but a very happy baby. It was a beginning step to teaching her intuitive eating, a skill I hope she has through her whole life.

During the toddler years we are given a wide-open window to teach our daughters about body love. The sole purpose of being a toddler is to grow and explore. Every single day during this phase offers us the chance to provide reinforcing messages about how incredible her little body is.

❈ It is so important to dress your little one in soft, nonrestricting play clothes that allow her room to move comfortably. Her brain and body are learning so much from the gross motor development going on at this stage.

❈ More teeth and hand/finger control mean more fun at feedings. Give her a wide menu, and continue to let her see you eating and enjoying your food. Try to avoid saying things like, "Good girl for finishing your plate," as that begins to teach her that her eating behaviors are "good" and "bad" and judged by others. Instead, focus on comments that target how she is feeling during eating, such as, "How does my girl's tummy feel after all of that tasty food?" Also, kids at this age are too busy to eat big meals, so providing lots of healthy, smaller snacks and meals is the key. Relate eating her food to giving her energy and power for her brain and muscles. I used to ask Amelia if she could feel her brain getting healthier and brighter when she would eat her veggies. She would give me a sly smile and wiggle her eyebrows, trying to "feel" her brain.

❀ Toddlers are usually moving during eleven and a half of the twelve hours they are awake each day. Provide her with many opportunities for climbing, jumping, running, rolling, sliding, swinging, crawling, dancing, and so on. As she is doing these things, keep the focus of your comments off how she looks while doing it and instead dial in on what she is accomplishing. Hear the difference between "Oh, my pretty girl is walking!" and "Where are those strong legs taking my walking girl today?"

❀ Allow her to make mistakes with her body, meaning let her get "stuck" and try to problem solve on her own. Not that a toddler necessarily needs to be taught independence, but this teaches her agency over her body, meaning she is learning that she initiates, executes, and controls her actions through the world.

❀ Toddlers in general are known for their wonderfully chubby bodies. Those round tummies and bubbly thighs are there for a reason. Unfortunately, this celebration of chub can sometimes be met with ire from people obsessed with their own weight. If you hear someone "fat talking" to your little child, be sure to immediately redirect the negative comment with a positive one about your daughter's healthy and growing body. A common remark is something like, "Enjoy those thighs now, honey, because it is the only time in life you get to look like that!" If it were my child, I would thank the observer for remarking on how healthy and strong my child is, and then walk away.

Preschool is such a fascinating time because now all of your parenting is put to the test as your little one ventures out into the world without you right by her side. A preschooler's ability to reason and think critically has grown, and this is such a great time to shape body image discussions and lay some serious groundwork for how your family will relate to your daughter's body.

❀ Being in control of her body is now a "thing," and this is usually expressed through the way she dresses. Preschoolers may have a different fashion sense than, say, everyone else in the world. There are few other times in life when it is appropriate to wear clothes with clashing patterns, a cape, a tutu, rain boots, and a Spider-Man mask to the grocery store. I am of the opinion that if her outfit is safe and appropriate for the weather, let her rock it.

Amelia spent most of her preschool days dressed like a Himalayan Sherpa, and it became her signature style. While there certainly were days I would have loved for her to put on the cute play outfit that I had lovingly set out, I allowed her veto power over my choices, and her Punky Brewster style allowed her to express herself. She was beautifully unself-conscious. And really, in five years will it matter that she insisted on wearing mismatched socks and brushed her hair every third day? In the big scheme of parenting, this seems like a smart battle to give up and allow the child some power.

❀ This is the age when kids really learn to tear it up on the playground, as well as do "big kid" things like learn to swim, ride a bike, and play sports. All of these things should be a part of her weekly playtime. Not only do these activities strengthen her body, they strengthen her sense of self and accomplishment. The idea that her body can do amazing things is important at this age. I remember the summer evening my dad took the training wheels off my bike and I rode down the street for the first time as an official two-wheeler. I remember my first jump off the high dive, and being taught how to climb a tree. I don't just remember doing these things; I can remember how I felt while doing them.

There are recreational sports teams for mighty mite-sized children to join, but team sports aren't necessary at this age.

Kicking a soccer ball with Mom and Dad at the park is just fine too. Show her how her body moves, the strength it has inside, and how fun it is to be healthy and active.

❈ Help her begin to deconstruct media messages. She may not get this right away, but it will teach her the beginning steps to critical thinking and media literacy. Question why the women she sees in advertisements all look the same, ask her if she thinks Barbie can be comfortable on perpetually pointy feet, ask her why the Disney princesses' waists are so small and their eyes are so huge. The aim isn't to make sure she gets her answers correct but rather to get her questioning and challenging the messages the media will be giving her about her body and how it should look.

❈ Preschoolers make excellent sous chefs, and helping with meal preparation is another step in teaching intuitive eating and having a healthy relationship with food. Talk about what different ingredients and spices do, why rhubarb is sour and strawberries are sweet. Focus on the taste, texture, and nutrition in food. Teach her about balancing nutrition and eating a rainbow of foods each day. Let her be in charge of the kitchen one night a week, and allow her to pick the menu and do as much of the food prep as she safely can.

Grade school is the time when your children will become more aware of body image issues, in themselves and others. My hope is that they remain strong and confident in who they are, but we all know that growing up involves some growing pains. They will most likely be teased at some point, and unfortunately the way a person looks or dresses is often the first thing attacked. We need to teach truly lasting lessons in this stage that give our children the sense of who they are, and which voices matter.

❈ This is the perfect age to introduce, if you haven't already, the idea of "inherited beauty," that beauty is passed down between the members of a family. It is not bought or found from a cosmetic bottle or diet product. We all have a genetic blueprint, and if we follow a healthy lifestyle, we look exactly how we are supposed to look. That may or may not match up with what the media is telling us about how we should look, but we need to teach our daughters to define beauty in our own terms. Maybe a nose or bust size doesn't look like the girls in the magazines, but it does look just like a grandmother or great-aunt, and she was a gorgeous woman. This also allows us to be proud of our various ethnic heritages, in case your Eastern European or Hispanic roots don't leave you looking like Malibu Barbie.

❈ My daughter looks a lot like me, but she also looks just like a great-aunt on my husband's Lebanese side of the family tree. I can remember seeing a family photo of my husband's family from the 1950s, and the woman in the center took my breath away. She was so pretty, and I remember telling him that if we had a daughter, I hoped the little girl would look like her. Amelia is proud of her dark hair and dark eyes. She likes looking at pictures of me when I was little, because we look so much alike. Around the house we have framed pictures of our family going back several generations. I show my daughter pictures of her grandmothers and great-grandmothers, aunts and great-aunts, and images of me that show all of us looking alike and looking beautiful and how we "should" look.

❈ Even if you are raising an adopted child, family photos are important. They show that we enjoy the life we have in our bodies through many years of the loving and joy that comes from being a family. You can focus on shared personal character traits and interests.

❈ Grade schoolers are most susceptible to teasing, as kids at this age start to etch out social hierarchy and the value of "fitting in." Talk to your daughter on a daily basis about how school and friendships are going. Ask questions that need to be answered with more than just one word ("How was school today?" versus "What was the best part about your day?"). If your daughter is being teased for some aspect of her looks or body, prepare and practice responses with her that she can use to deflect or stop the teasing ("I'm proud of the way I look" or "I don't worry about my looks, and neither should you"). Teach her the importance of not lashing out and being mean back, but rather showing her character as a strong and confident person.

- Teach your daughter how to be accepting of people's physical differences around her. What a person looks like has little to do with who that person is as an individual. There is much value in the old adage "Don't judge a book by its cover."

- Get her involved in some kind of sport or physical activity. Whether it is a team sport such as soccer or basketball or an individual sport such as dance or tennis, get her involved in something that teaches her about the power of her body. Martial arts and yoga are other great things to try. A recent study revealed that 80 percent of female CEOs had played a sport as a girl. Girls who play sports or are physically active are most likely to have a positive body image and take fewer physical risks with their bodies when they enter high school.

  Some sports can be a breeding ground for eating disorders, like dance, swim, cheer, and gymnastics. Weigh-ins and any focus on how the body looks while performing need to be closely monitored by parents, and a good relationship with a coach who cares about personal growth and skill development is key.

- Grade school is also an age when your daughter can start volunteering in the community, which will broaden her sense of the world and her place in it. The larger the view we have on life, the less likely we are to assume that life revolves around how we look.

- Get rid of or be prepared to be very guarded with your fashion magazines. Studies have shown just a few minutes of looking at a fashion mag can make a girl feel bad about herself. Switch your subscription to *National Geographic* or a cooking or woodworking magazine instead for topics the whole family can get in on, and get your fashion fix from blogs so that the emaciated and Photoshopped images on the glossy pages are not laying around your house. I once had a nine-year-old tell me, following an afternoon of reading *Vogue*, that if she can "pinch an inch" it is time for plastic surgery and that a tummy tuck was a girl's best friend.

❀ In addition to helping in the kitchen, your daughter can also help shop for and grow food at this age. An herb or vegetable garden is a great thing to have if you have the space, and shopping helps her learn additional skills including math and budgeting. A bowl of fruit on the kitchen table and easy access to healthy snacks allow her to make good choices for herself. Continue trying to eat meals together as a family (no TV!) and really use this time to engage with and learn from your kids. When I was growing up, we had family dinners all the way through high school, and it is still one of my favorite parts of my childhood.

❀ Be sure to have clothes that comfortably fit her growing and changing body and that continue to allow her to play and be active. I know a lot of young kids act like teenagers and want to dress like them, but a third-grader is still a little kid and needs to be able to act like one.

❀ Some girls may start to develop secondary sex characteristics at this age, as puberty seems to be happening earlier these days. Breast buds, weight gain and height increases, body odor, and the first signs of pubic hair all start to emerge around eleven to twelve years of age but can happen as early as eight or nine. Talk to her about the changes in her body, why they happen, and what they mean. Get comfortable talking about bodies and all of their parts. She has the right to know how her body works and to not be scared of or embarrassed by it. (Refer to the "What to Read" section in the Resources listed at the back of the book.)

Middle and high school years are hugely important for your daughter as she transitions into being a young woman and her social relationships become her focus. She is really going to need her support system as school becomes more academically challenging, friendships can get rocky, puberty is in full swing, interest in dating may appear, and life becomes uneasy again because she is transitioning from childhood to her teen years.

- ✸ Continue to be a role model for her with your own positive body image and healthy living. Cook meals together or try a new recipe once a week, take the dog for a walk together, run 5Ks together, and use language about your own body that you would want her to say about herself.
- ✸ Continue to have lots of healthy snacks and fresh fruit at the ready for your busy teen.
- ✸ Encourage her to stay in sports at this age, and any other extracurricular activities. Both help her gain confidence and a bigger picture of the world waiting for her, and both provide close-knit groups of kids who share a common interest and can be a support system when the rest of school gets rough.
- ✸ Share media together and discuss what you are seeing. Watch her teen programs like *Glee* or *Pretty Little Liars* together and discuss aspects of the show like body diversity (or lack thereof), decisions made by the characters, and how circumstances or consequences would be different in your family. Go to the movies together. Let her pick the music if you are working in the kitchen or yard together. You may not love her media, but what a golden opportunity to share that piece of her world, gain a better understanding of teen culture, and spend time together.
- ✸ A lot of teen media and music glamorizes alcohol use, drugs, and sex. Be a voice of reason when there is none, and respect that she is growing up and needs to know more than what the media is telling her. Establish what your family's values are on these topics, give her the information she needs to be a responsible young adult, and continue an open channel of communication on this. This isn't a one-time "We had the talk" scenario, it is many little talks and answering of questions.
- ✸ Make sure your spouse/partner is being respectful toward the family and others and not making negative comments about

women's bodies (whether it is real women you know or women in the media). This goes for siblings, too. Your teen is soaking in everything they are saying. Your home needs to be a fat talk–free zone.

❧ Encourage her to make apparel choices that leave her feeling confident about herself and show self-respect. If she walks into the family room in something you don't approve of or something that is provocative, try to resist telling her she looks awful or to take it off. Try meeting her halfway. Ask her why she likes the outfit, or what she is trying to project about herself with her clothing choice. Suggest she give some critical thought to how others might interpret her outfit, and how she is prepared to handle herself should unwanted attention or negative situations arise. These could include anything from being sent home from her part-time job to getting hit on by older guys. While the latter is inappropriate, she needs to be prepared to control her reaction to it so that she can walk away safely without further harassment.

We do stand a chance of raising girls who feel good about their bodies and whose interests expand beyond how hot or not they think they are. Especially when we start young and plant the seed early, we can teach our girls to reject what the media and culture impose on them. But first we need to get really honest with ourselves as parents, and do a gut check to see if we are living healthfully ourselves and if we are in any way contributing to her negative body image. It is a constant and daily fight, but it is one worth fighting.

How Body Image Affects Sexual Agency

Body image will also play a role in your daughter's sexuality as it develops. Her ability to feel and relate to her body, instead of objectifying herself to be judged by external sources, will make the difference between her feeling her sexuality, or performing it. When a young woman feels confident in her body and understands sexual agency, she is able to feel sexy and enjoy the intimacy of sex. When she needs constant external validation, we see dangerous patterns develop in which young women identify their worth by the level of attention or intensity of sexual interest they garner from others. This becomes an unhealthy cycle of self-objectification and robs her of the chance of feeling whole.

In *Reviving Ophelia: Saving the Selves of Adolescent Girls*, Mary Pipher makes an excellent observation (one of many in that book!) about girls and beauty:

> Girls who are too attractive are seen primarily as sex objects. Their appearance overdetermines their identity. They know that boys like to be seen with them, but doubt that they are liked for reasons other than their packaging. Being beautiful can be a Pyrrhic victory. The battle for popularity is won, but the war for respect as a whole person is lost. Girls who are plain are left out of the social life and miss the developmental experiences they most need at this stage of their lives. They internalize our culture's scorn of the plain. The luckiest girls are neither too plain nor too beautiful. They will eventually date, and they'll be more likely to date boys who genuinely like them.

When I was in high school, I felt a lot like the type Pipher describes. I was told frequently by all of the adults around me how pretty I was and what a great girl I was, and at the same time was told by the boys around me that I was too vocal and too hard to control and didn't make good girlfriend material. I felt trapped in this surreal land where I was told constantly by adults that I was "such a catch," but the reality was the boys my age were really only interested in me shutting up and putting out. I could achieve that sought-after teen girl status of "I have a boyfriend," I just had to change who I was as a person first. When I did casually date or have a sexual relationship with a boy on my own terms, I was called a slut, a whore, and a bitch by others (mostly girls). Yet when I denied these boys a hook-up or a blow job, I was called a slut and a bitch by the boys. And then I didn't quite understand the idea of having a boyfriend but remaining completely chaste because any amount of sexual activity on my part would earn me the branding of "whore." The boy, of course, was free to go. Talk about stacking the deck.

Robyn Silverman points out in her book *Good Girls Don't Get Fat: How Weight Obsession Is Messing Up Our Girls and How We Can Help Them Thrive Despite It*, high school girls who are sexually active and overweight (or who think they are overweight) are less likely to use condoms than normal-weight sexually active girls. When girls tie their body insecurity to their people-pleasing skills and bring those into sexual relationships, they put their own sexual and emotional health at risk.

Sex can be a really great part of life, and it is something that I want my daughter to enjoy in her adult life. It may be hard to think of your little girl that way now, but our job is not to preserve them as little girls; rather our job is to raise confident, content, and strong young women. I feel comfortable acknowledging the fact that my daughter will some-day be sexually active, and when she is, I want her to enjoy sex and enjoy her body having sex. What I don't want is for her to be so unsure of herself, or base her contentment about her looks on the amount of attention she gets from guys (assuming for the moment she is straight), that she makes dangerous decisions regarding sexual activity that leave her emotionally hurt, physically hurt, diseased, or pregnant. I want her to have confidence in her body, find herself beautiful inside and out, and enter her relationships as a grown woman ready for the emotional intimacy and pleasure that sex can bring to her life.

Start the Conversation

I get so many messages and e-mails from parents, aunts, and teachers about how to talk to girls about body image. These messages contain fear, hopelessness, and confusion. My answer is that if you are doing it, you are doing it right. There is no perfect way to go about this, you just do it. I have talked with many a teen girl who has told me her parents never talked to her about body image, media literacy, drugs, or sex. Honestly, it leaves me a little shocked, and wondering how the parents felt they could afford to *not* talk about these things with their teen. I suggest these three main goals when addressing these topics directly with our girls:

1. Reinforce to her that what media tells her about how her body should look is completely bogus.
2. Have her question why media don't tell her she is beautiful the way she is.
3. Build confidence and appreciation in her for the things her body can do, rather than what it looks like.

For those who need some conversation starters, I highly recommend *Body Language: Cultural Conversation Reaching Out and Reaching In* by Susan Russell. It provides a jump-start to discussing self-esteem, body image, media influence, and identity. Dr. Russell identifies great open-ended questions such as, "What words are used to describe girls?" "How does media help you feel good about yourself? How does it lower your self-esteem?" "What do you say to yourself when you look in the mirror? Does this help or hurt your day?" and many others.

Many Pigtail Pals parents have shared their real-life thorny situations and conversations around body image. One mother wrote, "My daughter and I were at a pool party and she was eating a bag of Doritos. She asked how many calories were in it and whether they were healthy. I'm not sure where this came from; she's six! I told her how many calories there were and showed her how to read the nutrition label. I explained that she's healthy, and chips in moderation are OK. I was left unsure whether I'd done the right thing discussing calories at such a young age. How can I teach my daughter healthy body image?"

My response to her was that, in that moment, I thought she did the right thing; she turned the conversation to quantifiable things like measurements of caloric energy and nutrition (as opposed to subjective, like, "Honey, you are nowhere close to being fat. Don't worry and just eat your chips." By answering the way she did, she taught her daughter to look at food based on energy and nutrition, not whether or not it will make her gain weight. I advised her to "continue to empower your daughter to read labels to see what ingredients she is really eating. Teach her about vitamins, minerals, lean protein, and whole grains. At six, she is old enough to make a list with you of everyday snacks that are healthy and once in a while snacks that are perhaps a little less so.

Then go to the store together and stock up on the everyday snacks, and place them in spots in the fridge or cupboard that she can reach."

Another mom who was worried about the unavoidable influence of things and people outside the family on her daughter's body image, wrote, "I have a nine-year-old daughter and have noticed no matter how hard we try at home, other kids impact her thinking a lot. She recently has started saying she is fat. She's barely been eating lately, and when I confronted her about what's going on, she said she's on a diet. None of this kind of talk is reinforced in our household so I'm not entirely sure where she gets it, but I was going to sit her down tonight and have a talk, and I want her dad to as well. Any words of wisdom how to handle this?"

I told her I thought sitting down with Mom and Dad for a talk about such a serious issue is a great idea, but it doesn't have to be a formal, intimidating conversation at the table. I suggested they could snuggle up on the couch, pile onto her daughter's bed, anywhere she'll feel safe and able to talk. Maybe younger siblings could already be in bed or playing with a neighbor so that she has her parents' undivided attention. Then, I advised:

> If it were my girl, I'd start by saying how much I love her and how proud I am of her that we can have these talks. I would ask her why she thinks her healthy body is fat and why she chose to go on a diet. Ask where she learned 'how' to diet. Most likely this is coming either from school or her friends, but it could be as simple as her reading the magazine covers in the checkout line and wanting to try things out. Assure her that no one is in trouble but that you need to understand where she got her information, because not eating can be very dangerous.
>
> If her body frame is like yours was as a kid, show her a photo of you from that age and show her she looks just how she should for your family. Bring up that you've noticed she is not eating, and why that concerns you—that a child her age needs to eat for her brain, bone, and muscle development. I would mention to her that at her last check-up, her doctor said her weight was healthy for her height, if that is the case. Suggest that instead of her being on a diet, you'd like her to help you come up with a list of twenty foods that make

her feel healthy and happy. Maybe #17 is donuts and #18 is broccoli, that's OK. Ask her how she wants to work these foods into the family menu. Invite her to be your helper at the grocery store, counting out and weighing produce. Ask if she'll help you plan meals. So pancakes, apples, cheese, yogurt, and strawberries were on her list of twenty? Could your family make every Wednesday the official pancake breakfast day? Could a cheese board along with fruit-and-yogurt parfaits be dinner some night?

Here's what you *do* want to do: express to her that you and Dad are concerned about what she has said and why she is not eating. As her parents, it is your sole responsibility to ensure that she is healthy. Find ways that work for your family that teach her food is a wonderful and enriching part of life.

Here's what you *don't* want to do: turn this into a control game. You can't forbid her to diet. You can't force her to eat or shame her or threaten her. You also need to try not to sigh or click your tongue when she says, "So and so's sister taught me blah blah blah," because you then just made that kid the coolest kid around.

I would ask her what she would like her body to look like, and if she gives an example of an adult, point out to her that she is a child and isn't supposed to look like magazine models at her age. Talk to her about your family eating healthy food and being active, and how the combination of those two things leaves her body looking just the way it should. If what she says continues to disturb you, considering she has already restricted her eating, I would share your concerns with your pediatrician.

There is no single correct way to teach positive body image to our daughters; approaches are as varied as displays of love. Positive body image is a form of self-love and one of the most powerful gifts parents can give to their girl. How a young girl thinks about and respects her physical self will impact some of the bigger decisions she will make as an older child and teen. As parents and caring adults we can ensure that she sees herself and her body as a gift that allows her to do many amazing things in life.

Letters from the Experts

Robyn Silverman

Robyn Silverman is a child and teen development specialist, professional speaker, and author who appears regularly on media such as *Today* and *Good Morning America*. She is the author of *Good Girls Don't Get Fat: How Weight Obsession Is Messing Up Our Girls and How We Can Help Them Thrive Despite It*.

Dear Parents,

When we look around at the thousands of media messages that fly in the faces of our girls each day, the task of "doing something" about it can seem overwhelming. What can we, as parents, say to combat such an aggressive collective ambush? Can we really make a difference?

As it turns out, yes we can.

It's true that media is an aggressive delivery system of sexualization, objectification, thinspiration, and body bullying. Every time we turn around it seems another ad, another TV show, or another magazine article is slated to get our daughters to buy into yet another way they are not good enough, thin enough, or pretty enough just the way they are. It's normal to feel frustrated and even defenseless against the rigor of these messages. But I'm telling you, as parents, we are more powerful than we realize.

We understand our children best. We demonstrate our values consistently, persistently, and insistently. It is we who see our children every day in routine life, but it is also us who they seek out in the wee hours of the night when things go wrong. It is our voices they hear when they are about to make a choice—right or wrong—and our actions they often mimic when they go out into the world.

This may seem scary, but it can be quite empowering. It means that we can speak our truth and help to create the recording that our daughters play in their heads throughout the day when they look in the mirror, walk the halls of their schools, and go out on dates. It means that we can show them what it looks like to be confident, assertive, and proud of who we are.

The question is, how can we deflect rather than reflect what society at large is dishing out? I say, if the media is going to be loud, be louder. If her friends offer a negative opinion, provide a positive perspective. If her own voice drags her down, pull her up. Commit to making one small change, as it is often slight alternations in approach, wording, or actions that can make the biggest difference.

She may act as if she isn't listening. She may tell you it doesn't matter. She may even argue with you about what you are saying. But, again, it will be your example she follows and in the wee hours of the night, it will be your voice she hears in the privacy of her own head telling her she is amazing just the way she is.

Warmest regards,
Dr. Robyn Silverman

Navigating Too Sexy Too Soon Birthday Parties and Holidays

Birthdays and holidays are supposed to be magical memory makers for kids. But they can also make the conscientious parent trying to avoid sexualization sweat. Should you let your daughter keep that doll she received as a gift that resembles a sex worker? What do you do if you're uncomfortable sending your five-year-old off to a "glamour girl makeover" party but all her friends are going? How do you respond when she's poring over a catalog of *children's* Halloween costumes that barely cover her behind? This chapter offers some tips for navigating these land mines and discussing them with your youngster.

The Holiday Attire Trap

For girls and women especially, a large part of holiday celebrations such as Christmas, Chanukah, or Easter is dressing up for the festivities. For little girls that means looking adorable in those irresistible crinoline-and-satin holiday dresses with fancy buttons and sashes, paired with patent leather Mary Jane shoes.

But before spending a sizeable dollar amount on a gorgeous holiday outfit that your daughter will outgrow next year, think about what messages these extravagant outfits send to our girls. The most important part of celebrating holidays is not about appearance or eliciting compliments from family about what a pretty little doll your daughter is. Holidays are about time with family, tradition, and renewing the spirit. Pretty dresses and dainty shoes may inhibit your child from playing, moving, dancing, and interacting as she otherwise would. Are the boys in the family wearing outfits that require them to sit quietly and play nicely? Or that hold them back from playing outside or wrestling with the cousins? Dressing up is fun and it does make for some cute family photos, but what a shame if those pretty dresses are keeping our girls out of the game because they (or you) are worried about wrecking the dress or getting dirty.

I have heard from several parents that they felt obligated to provide these decorative outfits for their girls, but after noticing it kept their daughters out of the action they began to pack tote bags with a change of play clothes and shoes. Or the girls wore gently used hand-me-down dresses and shoes so that when "running through puddles" with the cousins became the afternoon activity, the parents didn't wince over a hundred dollars' worth of frilly clothes dragging through the mud.

My favorite holiday memories as a kid are centered on running wild with my cousins. Let's look at other ways we can provide our daughters magical holiday moments that focus on experiencing joy and togetherness rather than on how cute and pretty they look.

Birthday Parties and Gifts

I get a lot of questions from parents relating to all things birthday, such as:

> "Can I include a gift wish list with our invitations to avoid receiving inappropriate gifts for my child?"

"What do I do with the awful sexy doll / kitten heels / bag of makeup that was given to my child?"

"What do I do when my kindergartener insists on buying a toy as a gift for a party she's been invited to that is so inappropriate, it is inappropriate to explain to her why it is so inappropriate?"

"We got invited to a diva rock star princess spa and 'cocktails' limo-fashion show party, for a five-year-old. What in the world!?"

"How do I handle my daughter being invited to a party with her fifth-grade friends where they plan to have a *Twilight* movie marathon?"

We celebrate our child's birthday because it is the day she joined our world, made our family that much more complete, and began the journey of life. We honor one more year of health and happiness under her belt and look to the coming year to be filled with more learning and exploration.

That, of course, is the poetic view of birthdays.

When you're a parent, you know there is the nitty-gritty side of birthdays: planning a guest list, invitations, cake and food, party activities, treat sacks, decorations, and so on. You can make it as simple or as complex as you want. You put a lot of effort into this day, and you want the best day for your child. This can be easily undermined when your child receives that gift that drives you up the wall and straight to the returns department. Every parent has his or her own different breaking point. For me, it is sexualized dolls. Another friend of mine abhors makeup for young girls. Yet another hates toys with batteries, or toys that are weapons.

To answer a question I get frequently from Pigtail Pals parents, I do not think it is polite to include gift suggestions with birthday party invitations. You sent out the invites because you wanted these people and families to come celebrate your child. If they do bring a gift, then how very lovely of them to do so. However, it is wonderful if a guest asks when they RSVP what would make a wonderful gift for the birthday girl. So be prepared! Make a list of toys, games, crafts, or books that align with both your child's interests and your values that you can supply to friends who are thoughtful enough to ask.

❀ Recognize what skills your child will be growing into during the coming year, and be ready to list a couple of items that reflect this. For example, a two-year-old during the coming year will be ready for finger paints and twelve-to-twenty-four-piece puzzles.

❀ Seasonal toys are great suggestions: bubbles, playground ball, mold for making ice blocks, or snow paint. Art supplies and board games are perfect and usually a good price for a gift.

❀ For older kids, have them help you create a list, and then you've also created the opportunity for that talk about how to show gratitude for gifts and what gifts are/are not acceptable for your family. For example, your daughter has invited over a classmate who is obsessed with all things Lady Gaga or Monster High, neither of which you want in your home. Take a preemptive strike and explain to your child that should she receive gifts that your family has deemed inappropriate, she can exchange or donate them. The importance of the day is having fun with friends, not getting stuff.

This is a two-way street, so if your child is invited over to a themed party that doesn't jibe with how you do things at your house, talk to her ahead of time about the focus of that day being on the birthday girl and not her decorations or her gifts. Different families have different rules, and we need to be respectful, especially when we are another family's guest.

For my kids, we have small birthday parties, but I try to have a list ready of ten to twelve gifts, and then I share one to two ideas per invited family if they ask. My group of mom friends is really awesome at asking what other children would like as a gift, and I just say something simple like, "We are so glad you can join us for the party! To answer your question about a gift for Amelia, she still loves all things oceanography and science related, and of course art supplies for her are always a hit." This approach also makes it easier for shoppers, especially if they bring their child along to help shop, they have more to work with should they not be able to find one item suggested. A suggestion like "art supplies" is very open-ended, and we've received everything from a garden stone decorating kit, to giant artist's sketch pads and the biggest box of crayons I've ever seen, to paints and beads.

The other problem with suggesting gifts on the invitation is that people may not think the same way you do. Asking for "age-appropriate, gender-neutral toys" may mean absolutely nothing to the guest. Instead I am very direct, and if they ask for gift ideas, I have a list of items at the ready and can give a couple of suggestions within a $10–$20 price range.

Speaking of families who do toys much differently than you: give them the benefit of the doubt. A family we know whose house is awash in all things pink / Disney princess / Tinker Bell / Barbie / Hannah Montana has been to many of my children's birthday parties and has never given us a toy that made me wince. We respect one another's differences, and their children have every single time picked a gift that honored and reflected my children's interests. In turn, when we give gifts to their children, my kids choose something great for them, like a fun science kit or art project, and then we wrap it up to look like it is fit for a diva with zebra-print paper, glitter spray on top of the package, and topped with a hot pink sparkly bow. There are many ways to be a girl, and we honor that.

If e-mailing the party details to your family is acceptable and expected practice within your clan and it is standard to make gift suggestions at that time, then who am I to rile you up? If that is how your extended family gets business done, that's fine and it is efficient. My family does that at Christmastime because we are scattered across the globe, and it just makes things easier when people are shopping and traveling between multiple time zones and continents.

I also think it is fine to request "No gifts please" and just enjoy a day of fun, and later on exchange a few gifts from family. Since birthday parties are really about celebrating the child, not hauling in gifts, another idea I think is cool that I learned from another mom is to ask that the attending children each make a gift for the host. She said they have received really cool craft projects, very sweet cards, and a few painted rocks for the birthday girl's garden. I thought that was a great way to teach kids about consumerism, crafting, the nature of giving, and the graciousness of receiving a gift from the heart.

What to do with gifts that drive you up the wall? Sometimes, despite all your best preemptive efforts, your child will receive a gift that you do not approve of. Amelia has received makeup that I wasn't prepared for or crazy about, but I let it slide because, after a day or two, it was forgotten. And makeup can be used artistically or for role-play during dress up, so it seemed to balance out. Had the gift been an inappropriate toy, video, or CD, we would have sat down and talked in an age-appropriate way about why her dad and I felt the gift in question was inappropriate for a child her age and that we would be happy to take her to the store to exchange it for a better choice.

Of course, it is kind of tricky to explain why something is so inappropriate when a kid this age shouldn't even be thinking about the inappropriate aspects of the inappropriate gift. I know there are parents who just scoop it up and toss it, but that doesn't allow your child the opportunity to learn or build critical thinking skills (unless your kid is two, then yes, pitch it). Better to explain why the gift won't be staying in your home, take the child with you to return it, and help her pick something that is a more appropriate choice.

Before you head to the store, have a short conversation about what are better choices and what price range you are working with. You might even want to write a list (or draw pictures for pre-readers) of three or four other choices. That way you have a visual cue to use if you need to refer back to the conversation. Put your child in the driver's seat and make it about her making a good choice, not you taking away a "bad" toy. That, my friends, is media literacy and critical thinking, and a little bit of budget managing to boot—necessary and wonderful skills to give your children.

All of this, by the way, also applies to when your child is the shopper, choosing a gift for a party he or she will be attending. Talk about what rules or limits the other family might have, and what the gift your child is choosing tells the recipient about their friendship. Any kid can buy the hottest toy off the shelf. But your kid is so awesome and such a good friend, she knows that the birthday girl plays board games with her family every Friday night, or that she loves art and horses. Work from there, and pick a gift that really honors who that child is as a person.

Sticky Conversations

If the parent of an invited guest asks or hints about getting a gift you absolutely do not want your child introduced to, it is appropriate to speak your truth and say something like, "We prefer to stay away from toys that are focused on beauty and shopping." This can be said much the same way someone says, "Actually, we are allergic to nuts" or "Would you mind taking your shoes off, please?" No big deal, not passing judgment, but this is just how we roll at our house.

Now, you've made your position on sexualization and stereotyping clear to your family and friends. You've politely suggested gifts you're comfortable with. You've spoken your mind in a polite way. But no matter what you do, your sister is determined to be the "cool aunt" who always buys the "hottest" toys or clothes or music for her niece. How do you impress upon repeat offenders that your child does not

> Make sure your child practices ahead of time how to receive and express thanks for a gift. Also, go over with your child how to react when she is the guest at a party and she sees a gift opened that your family has deemed inappropriate. At a party when she was six, Amelia pulled the birthday girl's mom aside to discuss needing to return a Monster High doll that had been opened! The mom agreed with Amelia, but I was still embarrassed. ✻

need, and you do not want in your home, the sassy kitten heels and miniskirt for your four-year-old or the new Eminem CD for your ten-year-old? Go easy and, as always, act with grace. Below are some possible approaches, but you will ultimately have to decide how best to approach the person since each relationship is so different.

"Aunt Midge, thank you so much for coming to Lydia's party. Yes, she loved seeing you and enjoyed opening your gift. Actually, since you brought it up, I wanted you to know that we decided to return Rhinestone Fashionista Barbie for a big floor puzzle. Well, I know you loved Barbie as a girl, but she's changed a lot over the years from when you were little, and you know how conscious we are about raising Lydia to be a confident girl. We prefer to stay away from toys that are focused on beauty and shopping. You should see Lydia stick her tongue out as she works on the puzzle. It is really quite darling."

"Amy, thanks so much for joining us on Saturday. That skit you did with the kids still has us chuckling. Listen, I actually wanted to discuss something with you, because I know how much you love being Maddy's auntie and how much she means to you. It's just that I've been doing so much reading about all of this sexualization stuff, like, you know, when girls grow up too fast, well, it just has John and me kind of baffled. We felt the bikini and high-heeled sandals that Maddy opened fell into that category. She's only five, so things like art supplies, dress-up clothes, puppets, books, you know, that is all so great for her. We love how her face lights up every time she sees you, and it felt really good to be able to be honest with you about this."

"Hi, Kate. Oh, Elise told Morgan at school that we returned the gift? . . . And oh, well, I'm sorry Morgan's feelings are hurt by this as certainly that wasn't our intention. We really appreciated you coming to the party, but Elise and I decided that the *Twilight* movies and T-shirt weren't a good fit for her right now. Yes, I know Morgan loves them, but she has older sisters so she is exposed to different things at your house. I think it is so great that Morgan loves monsters, and maybe next time the girls play we can help them set up a haunted house, or make life-size monster paintings."

Keep in mind that you are your child's chief advocate. But if speaking up will cause holy war with your mother-in-law, realize that family is more important that any imported plastic junk that will be forgotten in a matter of months. I believe in using media literacy with our kids and sticking to our values, but I'm not sure it's worth losing friendships or family relations over. And you can always say the dog ate it or that it got left behind at a restaurant. Lying isn't great, but little white lies for the sake of family peace are permissible in my book.

You have every right to say, "Oh no, that garbage does not enter this house." Each family has its different line in the sand—you have to decide where to draw yours. But don't draw it at the expense of enjoying your child's special day. These critters grow up so fast, and ten years from now, allowing one gift you disapprove of into the home won't seem like such a big deal. No single gift can undo years of good parenting, so relax, have some cake, and enjoy your kiddo smiling from ear to ear on her birthday.

Glamour Girl Parties

Here's a recent question I got from a mom:

My daughter handed me an invitation to a "glamour girl" party: "Get your hair styled, makeup, fingernails painted, sing karaoke, dress up, and put on a fashion show for your parents and friends." Ugh! Here's where this stuff gets hard. It's easy enough to keep it out of my house, but now what? So all of the other girls in her class go to this and she misses out and has to hear about it the next Monday? That's no fun. I'm not thrilled about the whole thing, but it's really the makeup part that bothers me more than anything.

So . . . thoughts? Advice? Insight? What's more educational, keeping her home and trying to explain why, or letting her go and then using it as a teaching tool for explaining my views on these things?

Usually held at a spa or beauty salon, "glamour girl" parties are the rage right now. Girls get vamped up with "sassy" hair, makeup, and nails. Sometimes they sip kiddie cocktails, sometimes they travel by limo. Sometimes they drink kiddie cocktails *in* the limo. The thing is, that scenario just described my sophomore year of college. Believe me, you don't want your seven-year-old reenacting my sophomore year of college.

This type of party sexualizes our girls in birthday party form and age-compresses them with the message that socializing around drinks and beauty treatments is what women live to do. Now, I love my glass of Pinot and mani-pedi just as much as the next girl, *but*, I am thirty-five years old. When I was seven I was excited to be allowed to drink a can of Orange Crush. If we let our daughters act twenty years old when they are in second grade, then what's left? Where do they go? What boundaries are there left for them to push?

Pampering can be fun, and birthday parties are supposed to be about being special for the day. But I've heard from many moms who were really upset by things that took place at spa parties: drinking fake cocktails, listening to inappropriate and sexually explicit music, the girls being handed a stack of magazines and told to pick out the pretti-est girl, a fashion show at the end of the party with the girls encouraged to strut down a runway and strike a sexy pose for the camera. There is also a great deal of sitting and waiting during the treatments when the girls don't really interact with one another. None of these sound like very uniting, beautiful activities to me. Of course "girl time" is qual-ity time, and important time. But spa parties like this also do another harmful thing: they leave out boys. So this hot trend is putting a kibosh on any coed birthday parties, and coed friends are important.

And yet, despite all this, how does a parent say no to her daughter's joining in on something that all her best friends might be participating in? It's a fine balancing act. Here was my answer to the mom in distress:

> I understand your discomfort. I suggest if you feel your daughter
> will be safe and well looked after, you let her go. The social aspect of
> the party will have a bigger impact on her than the makeup. Each

of us has a different line—for you it is makeup. I respect that. This is the kind of moment out of our control as parents that we can use to craft into a learning experience.

I suggest that before she goes, you explain to your daughter what a special occasion it is for her to get to wear makeup and do these fancy, big-girl things. Then you go over good manners for the party and send her off and tell her to have fun. When you pick her up, help to shape her takeaways about the experience with questions like:

"Was it fun to have to sit still to get your hair/makeup/nails done?"

"Did you want to sit still or wiggle around?"

"What kind of fancy, big-girl hairdos did the other girls get?"

"Were you able to count how many colors of nail polish? How did you choose your color?"

"Who sang the funniest song?"

"What kind of fancy outfits did you wear in the fashion show? Was the dress up the best part, or was the singing the best part?"

"This was a special treat, should we take a picture of you all fancied up? We don't do this often, and it would be fun to remember."

And you know? She's probably going to answer, "Mom, Riley got two of the same puzzles and her brother was there even though it said *no boys* and he ate more cake than us but the cake was good and Riley liked my present. . . ."

Just like a wedding, she's going to remember the cake and whether the guest of honor liked the gift. Save the makeup fight for another day.

I was happy to get her feedback after the party: "Melissa, I have to say, you hit the nail on the head. When I asked her what her favorite part was, she said, without hesitation, 'the cake!'"

Silliness, Fantasy, and Service Are "Girly" Too

Contrary to popular culture (and the new LEGO Friends sets!), there is more to being "girly" and girl-bonding than shopping, sipping drinks, and doing your hair and nails. Here are a few ideas for fun, creative parties that can even slip in a little salon-treatment fun too, but in a toned-down, DIY, and age-appropriate way.

- ❋ Have the kids put on silly, crazy dress-up costumes, roll out a giant piece of butcher paper, and then step in a tray of paint and dance while you blast music. Let them get as messy and act as crazy as they want. While the paint dries on their newly created mural, they can wash their feet in a big tub of suds, grab a towel and a juice box, and sit down to braid one another's hair. Because, you know, they are seven.

- ❋ For summer birthdays, try a birthday party at a campground. The kids can arrive in or bring their bathing suits and soak one another with squirt guns. Each girl can decorate a bag with puffy paint and use it later for a scavenger hunt. If facilities allow they can swim, tell ghost stories, roast marshmallows, open presents, and do the scavenger hunt.

- ❋ For winter birthdays, girls can put pretty sugar crystals on the whipped cream resting on top of their hot chocolates, sit at a beautifully decorated table, and peel and cut cucumbers for their eyes during homemade honey-and-cream facials. Afterward, have the girls cut little snowflakes from white, blue, and silver paper and write on them ways they are beautiful inside and out. Provide a bowl of ribbons so they can hang their snowflakes in their rooms.

- ❋ Younger girls might like a fairy-themed tea party birthday. At one we attended, the family had a pretty table set with a beautiful tea service, and the girls could choose flowing tulle skirts and head ribbons. After the children had gathered in the sunny yard, a "real" live fairy arrived to read stories, sing songs, and paint faces. The full-face butterfly the fairy painted on Amelia's face was exquisite. Amelia had stars in her eyes when I picked her up and she talked about that party for months. It was truly an afternoon full of childhood wonder.

❄ Get creative with party venues. Amelia's sixth birthday was held at our veterinarian's office! She loves science, and our vet loved that and wanted to encourage her. Each friend brought a stuffed animal and a toy doctor's kit, and the vet brought his golden retriever. He taught the girls how to do a check-up and then gave them a tour of the clinic. They put on surgical hats and gloves, looked through medical books, looked at X-rays and specimens, and then spent a disproportionate amount of time looking at X-rays of constipated cats. Fun was had by all, they spent the morning learning about animals and a field in the sciences, and then we went home to party some more over lunch and cake.

❄ We have had "service birthdays" in the past, and I know families who do this every year. Instead of gifts, ask guests for teddy bears and books, for example, that will be donated to the nursery at a local women's shelter; school supplies for a fall birthday; pet supplies for the animal shelter; or grocery items for the food pantry. There are also websites such as Kiva or Heifer International where your child can set up a gifting page to receive donations that go out as a micro-loan to families in need.

❄ Another great idea for a service birthday party is to have each guest bring a "birthday kit" for the local food pantry, complete with cake mix, icing, candles, fun napkins, streamers, and a card. Every kid should get to make a wish on his or her birthday, and this helps out a family with a tight budget tremendously.

Horrifying Halloween

When I think back to Halloween and trick-or-treating as a kid, I have great memories of tromping around the neighborhood in creative, homemade costumes. These days, Halloween is a little different. Most noticeably, girls' (and women's) costumes have become sexier and sexier. I frequently hear from parents that once their daughter reaches a certain age, about eight or nine years old, they have a really hard time finding an age-appropriate costume. I do not hear this same complaint from parents of boys.

So far my family has gotten through Halloween with great hand-me-down or homemade costumes, such as when Amelia was Dora the Explorer or the Headless Horseman. Benny, our preschooler, wanted to be "a nice, good witch" this year, so we happily purchased a witch hat, cut a hand-me-down black cape to fit his little body, and he added his froggy rain boots and a pot from the toy kitchen he filled with plastic lizards.

As the kids grow, we'll have less ability to have so much control. I volunteered at Amelia's school dance this year and was shocked at what some of the fourth- and fifth-grade girls were wearing. We're talking ten- and eleven-year-old girls wearing outfits that are better fit for a college party. One little girl's butt cheeks were exposed, her skirt was so short. Their parents would argue with me that these were the costumes their girls wanted, or this was all they could find in the stores. And they would be right; the selection of costumes for girls in the pop-up Halloween stores and big boxes leaves a lot to be desired.

Here's why this matters and why a simplistic "Well, just don't buy it!" response doesn't cut it. It matters because what girlhood looks like in the marketplace has changed drastically, and that change is doing damage to our girls. Girls are getting messages from every source that being sexy and hot should be their main focus. It's the damaging, cumulative effect of not just the Halloween costume but also the song on the radio, plus the commercials on TV, plus the magazine cover, plus the image on the billboard, plus the character on the TV show, plus, plus, plus. . . .

Why and how did sexy Halloween costumes become the norm? Around my town, starting in mid-August, the Halloween superstores move into vacant retail spaces with a short-term lease and a truckload of cheaply made costumes, all of which resemble some version of a pornified French maid uniform. This is true of child, teen, and adult costumes. The formula is predictable: tight lace-up bodice revealing a lot of boob (or, in the case of children's costumes, revealing their nonboobs), short petticoat skirt, knee-high socks or a pair of fishnets, and tall boots. Throw in a lollipop and pair of roller skates and you've got a 1970s adult film.

Actually, the whole pornography analogy isn't far off. In my local Halloween superstore, almost all of the costumes are from a company called Leg Avenue. On their website the costumes look well made; in the store they look thin and cheap. Leg Avenue also makes lingerie, burlesque costumes, club wear, and pasties. Some of their stuff is tasteful—very sexy and very adult. As a sex-positive adult, I can appreciate that. But what does it say that in three clicks of the mouse I go from their webpage selling pasties and burlesque booty shorts to one hawking Cutie Bug or Beautiful Butterfly costumes in children's sizes? The difference between the children's, teen, and adult costumes isn't much except for their size. They all comprise culturally coded wardrobe components that have historically signaled the sex trade. For a grown woman such costumes are often labeled "Sexy [fill in the blank]!" For kids, basically the same costume is downplayed as "Sassy [fill in the blank]!" Who do they think they're fooling?

Somewhere along the line, Halloween stopped being about scariness and fantasy and became a holiday of packaged sex. When every store you go into is carrying these sexy children's costumes, and has been for years, it stops being a one-season fluke and becomes a reflection of our culture.

What the market bears is a litmus test of our society, and right now the message is that no age is too young to be sexy when it comes to our girls. What message do we give to our children and our society at large when we let them play at dressing up like hookers and sex workers? Maybe all of these sexualized clothes and toys and costumes come with a higher price than any of us are comfortable admitting. When we purchase them, we become a part of the system that feeds off turning young girls' bodies into sex objects. That system is full of marketers and pimps alike; the flesh of our daughters is their currency. The average age at which a girl enters (usually by coercion or force) prostitution is twelve to fourteen. She can earn her pimp upwards of $100,000 a year because of the high demand for young girls in the sex trade. We hear horror stories of girls as young as six or ten being sold into sex slavery, and a line of men out the door waiting to rape her. Outraged? You should be, and it happens right here in America.

Our girls get the message that being sexy and sexually available is what society wants and expects from them, at ages when they are developmentally too young to understand it. These Halloween costumes also send the message to our boys that girls are just eye candy and sexual playthings. Equally disturbing are the sexually loaded messages that the costumes send to the group of teenage boys or adult man watching your neighbor's fourth-grader bounce down the sidewalk in her ultrashort Sassy Sacagawea costume.

Speak Up, Recycle, and DIY

With the pornification of children's Halloween costumes, can we still enjoy a great American holiday? Of course! We need to use our voices to change the way the marketplace looks, and we need to help our kids process what they are inevitably going to see.

First, as consumers, we have every right to tell a retailer that we do or do not like their offerings. Ask to speak to the manager, and let him or her know you are unhappy with the sexualized costumes they offer. Let management know you could not find anything appropriate for your family, so you are taking your dollars elsewhere (or making something at home). The management may well respond that there is nothing they can do, that "this is what Corporate sends us." The next step is to ask how to contact the district manager or customer relations department at the corporate office. An e-mail or letter may not change things overnight, but if enough parents would voice their frustration over their costume choices and use their dollars elsewhere, companies would shift production to things we *would* buy. That is, after all, their sole purpose for existing.

You can also take the approach of gathering like-minded neighbors or families from school and arrange a costume swap party at someone's home. I promise that your neighbors have great stuff in their closets, and what a fun way to spend some time with them. Throw in a little apple bobbing or pumpkin painting and make it an annual tradition. Call or write your local paper and tell them about it, and explain why you feel the need to do it. Have a letter to the local costume shop printed out and ready for signatures telling them why you hosted such an event.

Now, how to prepare your children for the inappropriate costumes they will no doubt see and want from stores and catalogs? This is tricky, because explaining the inappropriateness can feel, well, inappropriate. How do you explain to your second-grader why a costume is too sexy without broaching the concept of "sexy"? The explanations will change as your child grows. Many times it is easier to ask questions than have a formal sit-down conversation. Ask questions and start conversations with your child right in the store, where you have visual aids.

> Need some creative Halloween costume ideas? How about a character from a book, a famous person from history, a fun occupation, or a vintage athlete? If your kids are older, put "zombie" in front of anything and it works: zombie chef, zombie mail carrier, zombie businesswoman. Or spin the globe, then put together a costume resembling the native dress of the country you land in. ❋

For little ones, pointing out some of the other negative aspects of a skimpy cheerleader costume is not only truthful but a way of getting around talking about sexualization at so young an age. For example, point out how chilly a skimpy outfit would be. Or perhaps a given costume is too dark and presents a safety issue (the safety issue also works for really grotesque masks you don't want to find down in the basement late at night). If you live in the south and the chilly argument doesn't work, try explaining that the outfit is more like something she would wear to the beach, but not appropriate for trick-or-treating around your neighborhood. Try explaining that the costume isn't well made, and the seams and loose threads won't hold up through two Halloween parties, the parade at school, and a full night of trick-or-treating.

For older kids, ask questions that get them thinking about whether or not *they* think something is appropriate based on their own level of comfort and your family values. Some costumes will have some wiggle room—maybe all it needs is a cardigan sweater to cover bare shoulders and a bare back, or maybe add leggings and a cape to help disguise a short skirt on a costume your girl really loves. Turn a supershort dress into a tunic top worn over pants. We teach our kids a lot by meeting them halfway while asking them to meet us and using our family values and expectations to do it.

Some questions to ask:

"Do you think you'll be self-conscious in a skirt that short? Will you be able to run around and have fun?"

"I think that costume looks too grown-up for you. What parts of it do you like? Maybe we can come up with better options."

"I understand the other kids are all wearing these. They are not my kids. You are. Let's come up with something more creative. Do you want to be scary, silly, or something mythical?"

"I think this costume might send messages that you are too young for. Do you understand what kind of messages I am talking about? Do you think those are appropriate for someone your age?"

When I've talked to both kids and college students about these supersexy costumes, most of them say they do not like them but don't know what else to buy. So many people have gotten used to running to the store or shopping online at the last minute and buying something premade. Let's challenge our kids to be more creative than Ice Cream Cutie in a short petticoat skirt. Let's get some creativity back and see more of those great homemade costumes we grew up with. I don't sew, but I've never had a problem whipping costumes together for my kids. Include your kids in the decision-making and design process, and make a fun event out of what is really a big "No, I'm not buying you that" moment.

The other message we can send both our girls and the pornified Halloween industry by making our own costumes or buying appropriate versions is that we do not have to accept the narrow version of femininity that marketers suggest and that the idea "sex sells" doesn't sell for our kids.

Letters from the Experts
Lyn Mikel Brown

Lyn Mikel Brown is a developmental psychologist, a professor of education at Colby College, and the cocreator of the non-profit Hardy Girls Healthy Women. She is the author of five books, including *Packaging Girlhood: Rescuing Our Daughters from Marketers' Schemes*, with Sharon Lamb (winner of a Books for a Better Life Award) and *Packaging Boyhood: Saving Our Sons From Superheroes, Slackers, and Other Media Stereotypes*, with Sharon Lamb and Mark Tappan.

Dear Parents,

If you're reading this book, you already know that media and marketers are competing with you for the right to teach your little girl about what it means to be a girl and your little boy what it means to be a boy. Megacorporations have a lot invested in winning this battle. They're willing to spend money, lots and lots of money, to marketers who then craft just the right messages with just the right promises. Marketers study children to understand what will grab their attention and how to make it more difficult for you to point your children in healthier directions. They pay developmental psychologists to help them hone emotional hooks: humor, a visual delight, a promise of happiness, friendship, popularity, competency, or power. They use language like freedom, power, and choice to sell your children a narrow set of images and options. Make no mistake: neither the companies nor the marketers they employ have your child's health and well-being in mind. Their job is to sell products, period.

So what's a parent to do? There are paths through the media forest of pink diva princess shopping hotties and tough violent slacker players. You can raise a media-savvy child who can learn how to make his or her own way through the pre-packaged world that marketers are trying to sell. It takes some mindfulness and a little effort, but what's new? You're parents. You're up to this. And you have a powerful secret weapon, one marketers are trying desperately to imitate: a genuine, trusting relationship with your child.

Everyone knows that relationships deepen when people engage in real conversation. The next time you're walking through the girls' or boys' departments of a clothing store, browsing the "blue" and "pink" aisles of any toy store, or watching commercials between their favorite cartoons, ask your daughter or son what they like and why they like it. Don't judge. Really listen. You may be surprised. Only when you understand where your child is coming from can you have a real conversation about their desires and your concern about the impact of media on those desires. Ask questions and reflect on what they tell you. Share your thoughts and feelings. Wonder aloud about more general media patterns you see and why they trouble you. You are preparing the way for those inevitable times when you'll draw the line; when you'll need to explain why there are things you don't like or won't allow, as well as what you do like about the alternatives you offer.

If you question, they'll learn to question. If you model conversations that feel genuine and inclusive, they'll learn how to talk with you and trust you to help them think about the media messages all around them. Simply by asking questions ("Why so much pink? What about the other colors we like?") or talking back to TV ads ("Geez, Mattel, why don't you ever show boys and girls playing together with that toy?"), you can open your children to new possibilities and model a way of seeing and talking about the narrow options presented to them. Help them notice when their world is becoming smaller and more limited, so they can step back and say, "That's silly. Real girls and boys aren't always like that."

One thing's for sure: you can't fight the power of media messaging by simply saying "No. Bad. Over my dead body." Not when media and marketers are saying, "Yes! Good! Now! More!" Of course, set limits that make sense to you. But remember to use your secret weapon. There will soon be a time when you aren't with them, when they're at a birthday party, shopping, or at the movie theater with friends, and they have to make their own choices. If you've helped them develop a vocabulary and a way of reasoning and talking about media, you have given them skills for a lifetime.

In solidarity,
Lyn

Getting Your Kids' Educators and Health Care Providers on Your Side

"You are such a good girl, let's get you a dinosaur. Here you go. Oh, wait, let's get you the pink one. Do you want some princess stickers too?"

"Here are your supply boxes, class. Pink is for girls and blue is for boys. Please go choose a box."

"We'll need two jump castles, a princess one for girls and animals or sports for boys."

"Did you catch this cold because you've been kissing too many boyfriends?"

"My goodness, you've really grown up since your last checkup. I bet the guys at school are all over you!"

All of the above statements have been made by teachers or doctors to my child or shared with me by members of the Pigtail Pals &

Ballcap Buddies community. In the case of the pink dinosaur, the doctor literally took a green toy dinosaur out of my baby daughter's hand and replaced it with a pink one, saying she would like pink better. She was thirteen months old. I assured him since she was a baby that the green one would have been just fine; she had not yet formed any gender stereotypes.

I have to bite my lip every time adults think they are offering children a choice when there is really no choice being given or the choice has already been made for the child based on the child's gender (or rather, the adult's assumption of the child's gender and how the child expresses it). It reminds me of a Henry Ford quote from his 1909 autobiography: "Any customer can have a car painted any color that he wants so long as it is black."

Parents have a hard job, and we need backup from the professionals who will interact with our children as they grow. I have a huge amount of respect for teachers and doctors, education support staff and nurses. The staff at my daughter's elementary school is amazing, we could not be happier with her teachers and the staff as a whole. We love the staff at my son's Montessori preschool, too. Last year we switched to a pediatrician who shows my kids so much respect I want to hug her every time we visit. Her nurses are equally awesome, and my kids talk about our doctor as if she is one of the family. We are fortunate to have this circle of professionals around our family because it hasn't always been this way. We have had experiences when teachers and doctors have introduced and reinforced gender stereotypes to my young children, and it drives me batty.

Before I became a parent, I was under the illusion that people whose occupations revolve around children were by and large child development experts who always had the child's best interests in mind. Since becoming a parent, I have learned that these professionals I hold in such high esteem are regular members of our society, make mistakes just like you and I, and are not always the kid mystics I had regarded them to be. The fact is that they are surrounded by and may have adopted the same gender stereotypes and bad habits all the rest of us are exposed to.

This chapter is your tool kit for working with health care workers and educators to get them on board with keeping childhood spaces free of sexualization and gender stereotypes. Any time we ask someone to challenge the stereotypes they project, it can feel awkward because we are asking them to push their comfortable thought boundaries and, frankly, we are telling them they are doing or saying something wrong. I do not want to focus on what these professionals are doing wrong but, rather, on how they can do things right. Because their work touches so many children and families, it is important that those of us who are fighting the gender stereotypes and sexualization of childhood reach out to these professionals with our message.

At the Doctor's Office

Some experiences that I have had with my own kids have really frustrated me. I teach my children to respect teachers and medical professionals, yet on more than one occasion Amelia had to call these professionals on their use of gender stereotypes during the course of their job.

One time we were being seen by a pediatrician new to our family, and he greeted my then–preschool-aged daughter by asking if she had a boyfriend at school. It was the first thing he said to her. She was confused by his question, because we had been teaching her at home that boys and girls are just buddies when you are little, and boyfriend/girlfriend stuff is for teenagers. She answered that no, she did not have a boyfriend. The doctor, continuing to think he was being cute and funny, then asked if she at least had an ugly boyfriend. I was really annoyed with his antics but did not need to say anything because Amelia told him in a very direct manner, "No, I go to school to learn."

I know the doctor was just trying to be friendly, but for a guy who makes his living treating child patients, he did not demonstrate to us that he knew how to converse with my young child. Doctors are in a position of trust and respect from both the parent and the child. He or she is the keeper of children's health, a vested partner in their growth and healthy development. This includes sexuality. Whether she is four or fourteen, the first question my daughter is asked by her doctor should not be the status of her love life and whether or not she has a boyfriend, because then she is made an object, someone else's possession. She has been asked nothing of herself. Her amazing, vibrant, shining, talented self.

We managed to get through the appointment just fine, and then, sure enough, Amelia was rewarded with the default princess stickers she is routinely handed at the end of office visits. She wasn't given a choice: the nurse saw that she was a girl and made the choice for her: girl = princess. Amelia, at the age of four, would have preferred Scooby-Doo or a dinosaur or a fish. The problem when doctors' or dentists' offices and the like have these licensed character stickers or toothbrushes is that it is easy to fall into the "This is for boys/That is for girls" trap because so much of the children's media is divided that way.

We much prefer how our dentist does it. In the corner of the exam room is a treasure chest full of mostly gender-neutral little childhood goodies, and the kids get to make their own choice. The kids also get to pick stickers for their shirts during the dental exam, and on many occasions Amelia has come out with dinosaurs and Diego stickers, and her little brother Benny has emerged with Angry Birds and kittens.

Another time, Amelia was chatting up the general surgeon who had removed my gall bladder and asking her all kinds of medical questions during my post-op visit. Amelia was five years old at this point, and was fascinated by the process of surgery on the human body. During the conversation a photograph on the wall caught Amelia's attention, and a whole new line of questioning began. The photo was of my surgeon operating on a man in Africa whose arm had been severed in an accident. The photo didn't leave any details in question, and Amelia was riveted. She asked my doctor incredible questions, and the doctor complimented her, saying she thought we had a budding general surgeon on our hands. I really appreciated how the doctor showed Amelia respect by answering her questions thoughtfully and not brushing her off as a silly kid. The surgeon said she was very impressed with Amelia's hunger for science.

And like a script, in came the well-intentioned nurse to reward Amelia for her good behavior with two Disney princess stickers. Here my child had been quizzing a general surgeon for twenty minutes on anatomy, organ function, and surgical procedures in a field hospital, and she was rewarded with a character on a sticker whose body with a thirteen-inch waist flies in the face of all the medicine she was just so captivated by. Not to mention, I bring my daughter to the doctor to safeguard her health, and I do not need her being given items with characters that reinforce the thin ideal and eating disorders. Ironically, guess where I would take her if I felt she had an eating disorder? Yes, that's right, the doctor's office.

How best to navigate these two situations? With the boyfriend comment, Amelia fielded that one beautifully on her own. I encourage her to speak for herself and advocate for herself, and I did not feel her answer was bratty or discourteous to the doctor. She said what needed to be said, so I let it lie. I want her to know her voice matters, and while some may disagree, I think children have the right to correct adults when adults are being rude or inappropriate.

Had she been sitting there in uncomfortable silence, not knowing how to answer the doctor, I might have said something to ease the situation for her along the lines of, "You know, Dr. Smith, Amelia goes to school to learn and be friends with all of her classmates, boy and girls. She is most interested in art. Maybe you could ask her about the latest project she has made." A comment like that reinforces to Amelia the messages we teach her at home, and at the same time allows the adult to redirect their comments to the child.

Below is a list of questions the doctor could have used to get to know Amelia better and allow her to share about who she is as a person and things she can do. Parents can use this list to gently redirect health care professionals who are falling into what they think is cute "girl-talk."

- ❀ "How old are you?"
- ❀ "Know any good jokes?"
- ❀ "What is your favorite color?"

- ❊ "Why is blue your favorite color?"
- ❊ "Why do you think your baby brother is using his head to push the stool across the room?"
- ❊ "Did you see the funny poster of the babies in the flowerpots?"
- ❊ "How high can you jump?"
- ❊ "What is your favorite toy to play with?"
- ❊ "Did you make an art project in school today?"
- ❊ "What kind of silly things do you do with your family?"
- ❊ "What things do you do with your friends?"
- ❊ "Can I hear you count to twenty-five?"
- ❊ "Can you touch your nose and rub your tummy at the same time?"
- ❊ "What is the funniest thing you saw today?"
- ❊ "Have you been growing? Would you like to help me measure how tall you are?"
- ❊ "How fast can you hop on one foot?"
- ❊ "What is your favorite animal?"

In a situation like the one in which the nurse handed Amelia princess stickers because she was operating on a gender stereotype, I think the best thing to do is use it as a teachable moment for your child about manners and grace. It was, after all, meant to be a kind gesture and nothing is gained by embarrassing people. Your child has the option of accepting the stickers and saying thank you, declining the stickers and saying no, thank you, or saying as politely as she can, "I do not care for princesses, may I please make a different choice?"

> Every chance we get, we should take the opportunity to show our daughters how to speak up and advocate for themselves. ❊

If you go the yes, please / no, thank you route, talk with your child afterward about how the situation made her feel and ask her some critical thinking questions: Why did the nurse assume she liked princesses? Do all girls like princesses? What are some other things girls like? What would be some fun designs or pictures to see on stickers besides a cartoon character?

When you allow the child to ask for a different choice, you are teaching her that she doesn't have to accept being stereotyped or boxed in. She has the right to voice her opinion and make her own choices.

Sure, stickers at a doctor's visit might not seem like a big deal in the long run, but using your voice is like exercising a muscle. Strength comes from repetition and practice. And sometimes stickers at the doctor *are* more than just stickers, they're emblematic of the dozens of stereotypes that barrage our girls every day and are worth speaking up about.

Most medical offices order their stickers in bulk with popular children's characters on them. SmileMakers is the top vendor for these, and when I browse their website it looks as though most offices would order something like the $153 sticker sampler that includes a selection of thirty different design themes. When I look at the designs on the stickers, there is nothing that marks any particular stickers as "boy" or "girl." It is the preconceived notions the adults have dispensing them that mark which sticker your child is given. I say, let the kids make that choice. Girls can like Diego and dinosaurs just as much as boys can like Winnie the Pooh or Tinker Bell. SmileMakers has an enormous selection on their website, including many fantastic stickers for kids with no licensed characters on them, and you can always encourage your doctor's office to purchase those. You can also make the suggestion to your doctors that they carry rewards that are a little more gender-neutral, and get away from the characters that typically divide kids by gender. Oriental Trading Company and similar vendors offer all kinds of rings, little rubber ducks, bouncy balls, and little novelty toys that are great for all kids. And of course, there are small businesses like Pigtail Pals that offer stickers that respect childhood and have no hint of gender stereotypes or sexualization.

Doctors' and dentists' offices are usually scheduled pretty tightly during the day, so visits may feel rushed and not the right time to bring up with the staff a situation in which you felt that your child had been stereotyped. We need to be respectful of the office's schedule and the other patients waiting. My guess is that this issue is not something the office staff has thought of before. If you have the nurse's or receptionist's attention for a minute, you can say something simple like, "Thanks so much for helping us today. I wanted to mention that it would be great if the staff let the children choose their own stickers. My daughter really loves Spider-Man, and she feels frustrated when she is offered only Disney princesses because she is a girl. Kids have so many different interests, and they love being able to make their own choices."

That might plant a seed, but that seed may not grow much beyond the one person you speak to. Another option is to write a friendly letter directly to the doctor or dentist, and ask that he or she speak to the staff about not stereotyping their patients, and instead offer a little basket or handful of choices to choose from. Describe how kids are taught "boy" and "girl" choices, and how that puts a limit on childhood and who these kids can be. Explain that kids look up to doctors and nurses, and when those people reinforce gender stereotypes, it teaches the children those stereotypes are correct or the "right way to be." But if the staff could offer the children a selection to choose from, the child gains the opportunity to let her interests and personality shine through to people she admires.

Incidentally, these same lessons transfer to restaurants. The number one complaint I hear from parents in this arena concerns the age-old "Girl toy or boy toy?" question for that McDonald's Happy Meal. Some kids can shrug this off, but others have their feelings hurt by this question. McDonald's registers are actually keyed for "boy toy" or "girl toy," and to create a change in how they offer Happy Meal toys would require a massive internal systems change in addition to retraining thousands of employees. It is not an impossible change, but it is probably not happening any time soon. The best thing a parent can do is rephrase the question to the child in a way that is more respectful: "Honey, would you like the *Madagascar* toy or the Barbie toy?" I do advise that you not be rude to the employees, as they are simply doing a job the way they were trained. After your meal, you can always approach the manager on duty and suggest they offer the toy by name, not assumed gender.

While McDonald's is not the only restaurant to offer toys with the children's meal, many other fast food restaurants offer one toy for all children. McDonald's seems to be the most frequent offender in terms of segregating toys by gender. You can write or call the corporate office, but as many locations are franchised and owned locally, you might make more progress by speaking to the local manager, who has a pulse on the corporate culture and also a vested interest in providing a positive dining experience to align with values of the local clientele.

Step Up on the Scale

Another situation that can arise at the doctor's office is a nurse or doctor making an insensitive comment about your daughter's weight. Now, my children are both tall and thin for their ages, just like I was as a kid. Every time Amelia has been weighed at the doctor's office, the nurses have made some kind of awesome comment like, "Say, forty-eight pounds! Good job, sweetie! That's a big, healthy girl!" or "You are doing a great job of growing into a big kid!" Our nurses have always equated the children's weight to growing and being healthy and have never said words like "skinny" or "skinny Minnie" or "lucky to be thin." I appreciate our pediatric nurses reinforcing the message we give at home that Amelia is growing just right for her body. When the nurses phrase it as a part of doing the job of growing, a concept all kids are dialed into, they help each child understand she is an unfinished masterpiece.

I appreciate this not only for the sake of Amelia's personal body image but also because she gets the message that there are many different ways to have a healthy body. Some kids shoot up like weeds, some hang onto their baby chub a while, some have thicker builds, and some are just plain overweight. Certainly childhood obesity is a critical health issue in this country and not one to gloss over. But I have heard from parents about situations where their nurses and doctors haven't been as thoughtful about body image, weight, and a child's feelings as my pediatrician's staff. I have two friends who are in their midthirties now who were between the ages of eight and ten when their doctors told them they needed to lose weight because of a BMI index or the doctor being able to "pinch an inch." Both women are able to describe that exact moment to me with great detail and both believe it was the catalyst that put the wheels in motion for their subsequent eating disorders.

Said my friend Jennifer, "I can still remember standing on the scale and hearing the doctor tell my mother that I was overweight and needed to go on a diet. At eight years old! A diet! Up until that moment I had no idea there was anything wrong with my body. I left that appointment devastated and in tears. Almost thirty years later I can remember that appointment vividly because it was turning point in how I viewed the way I looked."

Jennifer is now a mother to her own little girl, a vibrant and feisty preschooler whose doctor told Jennifer he would feel more comfortable if the girl lost about ten pounds. Jennifer firmly disagreed (the child is healthy and active with a steady growth chart), but she didn't have much time to think about it because soon after this appointment some prior health issues caused Jennifer's daughter to become seriously ill and to lose about ten pounds. The child's new set of doctors were concerned about her weight loss and expressed to Jennifer they didn't want to see her lose any more weight and to try to gain back some of those pounds. D'oh! Thankfully Jennifer's daughter made a full recovery and is back to her vivacious, active, tall-for-her-age self!

Another friend of mine, Leslie Goldman Alter, a body image expert and women's health writer, shared with me a similar experience. She explained that when she was in fourth grade she was "chubby, due to an undiagnosed hypothyroid condition (still on medicine to this day for it)." She tried all sorts of crazy diets, eating only lettuce for a day, or making herself run around the block two times. "Obviously," she says, "nothing made a dent. So while at the doctor for a checkup I asked my beloved pediatrician if he thought I needed to lose weight. All I desperately wanted to hear him say was, 'No, you're perfect the way you are.' And what he did—not in a cruel or malicious way, I believe— was lift my denim top up a bit, sort of pinch the roll of skin/chub around my belly, and said, 'You could lose ten pounds.' It just killed me. I remember it like it was yesterday, and I'm thirty-six. In college,

I developed an eating disorder and then struggled with anorexia and bulimia for years after. I don't think the incident is what made me have an eating disorder on its own, but it was a trigger and helped kick the wheels in motion."

When a doctor makes a misplaced comment about size or needing to lose weight in front of a child, it is certainly appropriate to speak up for your child and say something like, "Zoey is a healthy eater and likes to try new foods. We love that she enjoys running around outside with her friends, and has a blast on the soccer team. We are proud of the healthy girl she is, and if you have any concerns, you are welcome to call me later this evening."

I asked Marci Warhaft-Nadler, author of *The Body Image Survival Guide for Parents: Helping Toddlers, Tweens, and Teens Thrive* for some tips on how a parent can navigate a situation with an inconsiderate doctor. She suggested, "If you're in a situation where your doctor brings up the subject of weight in front of your child, try to cut them off quickly by saying something like, 'We try to eat healthy and get lots of exercise, maybe you and I can chat more about that at another time.'" Warhaft-Nadler points out that nothing good can ever come from discussing your children's weight in front of them, and this includes conversations with their doctor. Hearing they are overweight from anyone is hurtful, but hearing it from someone in a position of authority like a physician is beyond damaging, she says. "Children aren't the ones doing the grocery shopping or scheduling activities. Therefore it's up to their parents to make whatever changes in the family's diet and/or level of physical activity that may be required." She notes that "The doctor's office can be an intimidating place for kids, and to have their weight discussed will just make them feel that there is something wrong with them. The last thing parents want is for their kids to feel self-conscious or ashamed of themselves for any reason. A much better idea would be for a parent

> It is perfectly acceptable to suggest to the doctor that a conversation be tabled during the appointment, and discussed between the two of you at a later time. ❋

to schedule an appointment with the doctor on their own to talk about ways they can help their son/daughter be as healthy as they can be."

Your pediatrician and his or her staff will be a part of your family for years. Find a doctor who is a good fit for your family. It is OK if you have to try out a couple different doctors until you find that fit. Help to create a relationship in which you and the medical professionals your child encounters work as a team, which means you being respectful and honest toward them and they toward you. If something happens in their offices that bothers you, let them know. They work in these positions because they want to help children, so give them the feedback that may be needed to allow them to do just that.

At Day Care and School

Depending on your child's age, school may be the place where she spends the majority of her waking hours. Five days a week she needs to navigate situations with teachers and classmates without the immediate help of her parents. She'll need to stand up to peer pressure, possibly bullying, and maybe even sexism from teachers. She'll also build wonderful friendships, begin the foundation of her educational career, and carve out a space in the world that is just hers.

When I sent my daughter to school, first two years of preschool, then off to public school, I was both excited and nervous. She was a happy and funny little girl who loved to learn and play. I was excited for us to have reached this stage of her childhood. I was nervous about the gender stereotypes and possible bullying she would encounter. She loved dinosaurs and spiders and getting messy while painting. Volcanoes made her giddy. Would the little girls include her in their play? And was I being judgmental toward these little girls thinking maybe they wouldn't include my child? Would the teachers recognize and accept Amelia as an individual or would they lump her into a "girl" category of pink sparkles and fairy wand crafts?

To be honest, we experienced a little bit of both. We made great friends, and at the same time were excluded from a princess birthday party because the mom thought Amelia wouldn't like it and wouldn't know what to do. Amelia had a preschool teacher who loved her quirkiness and brought in a giant floor puzzle of the ocean to show Amelia how life changed after her beloved volcanoes helped to form the Earth. She also had a teacher who suggested during a meeting that we get two different jump castles for the school picnic, a sports theme for boys and princess for girls. (Of course I asked what would happen if boys wanted to go into the princess jump castle!) Our kindergarten teacher loved when Amelia brought in one of her toy whales to present to the class.

On the other hand, at five years old Amelia once brought home a pack of Bratz playing cards as a prize for good behavior, with images on them that could accurately be described as "prostitute chic." She passes by myriad Barbie and Monster High backpacks hanging on hooks in the hallway as she walks to gym class, getting the message that she should be looking up to a narrowly defined beauty standard of thinness and sexiness, only to arrive at the class, where her gym teacher encourages both boys and girls to play hard and use their strong muscles. Thank goodness for gym class.

School, specifically public school with fewer limitations on commercialization and less likely to enforce a rigid dress code, becomes a perfect blend of contradictions. Girls are supposed to be working toward academic achievement while their classmate the next desk over wears a T-shirt that claims her favorite subjects are "shopping, lip gloss, and boys." Certainly a girl can be very smart and like those things too, but the constant gendering and sexism undercuts what should be healthier messages.

I've had parents complain to me about teachers who greet every girl student with a "Good morning, Princess!" and who separate boys from girls for different art projects, discourage cross-gender friendships, provide gender-coded pink and blue supply boxes for students, use posters or books in the classroom that perpetuate gender stereotypes, and subtly discourage their daughters in math, science, and technology. I know families who seek out charter schools or Montessori schools, or even decide to homeschool in part to avoid some of these issues. There are valid reasons for exploring those alternatives, but I also know many families, like my own, for whom, financially or otherwise, those options are not possible or preferable. Whatever school environment we choose for our children, it is up to us to instill the resiliency and critical thinking skills they will need to unpack some of the experiences that are bound to come up.

The Sanford Harmony Program (SHP) does tremendous work researching and writing about the importance of collaboration, friendship, and understanding between boys and girls as they pass through childhood. The goal of their school curriculum is to have children, parents, and teachers view gender through a different lens and make a difference in the way boys and girls see and treat one another.

I asked Stacie Foster, project director at the SHP, to comment on kids using critical thinking skills at school in order to break down the gendered or sexualized messages they might come across. She pointed out that teachers and parents are in a powerful position to guide children to recognize overgeneralizations and realize that the correct answer is usually not "all" or "none." For example, she says, "the message that 'boys like sports' should be noticed and challenged so that children have the opportunity to really think about this message and what it means. Do *all* boys like sports? Do you think there are boys who don't like sports? Do girls like sports? Some boys do and some boys don't, and there are girls that like sports too."

Similarly, Foster says, "we want children to understand that there is variability within individuals—sometimes a child may want to play sports, sometimes he/she may not. When children are consistently encouraged to recognize variability, they are better able to explore their interests and preferences outside of the confines of stereotypes and avoid making rigid assumptions about others."

"We see the gender divide far too often. It undermines kids' ability to view every other kid in their class as a potential buddy when they are sent the message that they are different from each other."—Hillary Manaster, Sanford Harmony Program ❀

In the classroom, gender should not be salient. Primary-colored supply boxes over pink/blue assignments based on sex, encouraging cross-gender work groups and friendships, and nipping teasing and bullying in the bud when they start up are all important in ensuring our children grow and learn in the healthiest environments possible. Some schools have policies against commercialization in the classroom, such as forbidding licensed character apparel and backpacks or apparel with logos. Most schools have dress codes, but many are subjective and are only useful if enforced. Schools that do have dress codes need a balanced approach to enforcement that does not target or shame girls.

Especially in preschool and early elementary when children are still learning how to be both friends and students, it can be hard for the little ones to understand why a student would be mean to another child or why a teacher isn't being fair about color choice or seating choice. My own kids struggle with understanding why another family might allow something that our family finds inappropriate. You can navigate much of this by discussing your own set of standards for your little student. This gives you the opportunity to sort through experiences based on your family values and use critical thinking to understand (and respect) why other people make different choices. This will also become an invaluable skill when your child is older and spending more time with peers than family.

These will adjust as our kids grow, but for the preschool and elementary years, our family's school standards go something like this:

- School is a kid's job. It is the opportunity each day to go to a place to learn with friends.
- We dress for school in a way that has us ready to learn and play.
- You do not have to like everybody, but our family acts like a friend to everyone.
- You are expected to be a leader, and if you see a student being teased or hurt, be a problem solver and not a bystander.
- Different families make different choices. Be respectful of differences, and respectful of our family's choices.

Whether she is six or sixteen, these standards will apply to my daughter. These rules have helped with everything from allowing Amelia to choose her own outfits for school to dealing with annoying or rude classmates to stepping in when a buddy was being teased for wearing a certain color to understanding why some parents allow things that aren't allowed at our house (like a bag of a dozen Oreos for snack break or a child wearing revealing clothing in the classroom).

Amelia's outfits never match. But she feels confident about how she is dressed, and if an outfit is appropriate for the weather, I let her wear it. I have worried about her being teased for her eclectic fashion sense, but thus far her classmates seem to be accepting of her style. She wears dinosaur or whale shirts with skirts and tights, and then clashing leg warmers and mismatched socks. She also refuses to brush her hair, and often looks like a brunette Medusa. Again, her classmates just accept that as part of their Amelia.

There are a few girls in her second-grade class, despite being the tender age of seven, who have already developed insecurities about how they look and dress. Some of these girls demand clothes from only a certain store at the mall, while others are learning this fashion and appearance obsession from their mom or older sisters. My daughter has no concept of brand-name clothing, yet she has some classmates who wear only designer duds or shoes. This can be a source of teasing for kids, and especially among older kids. I make sure that Amelia hears me complimenting other women, so she gets in the habit of seeing fashion as something to be enjoyed together rather than as a competition.

Every once in a while, as we're sharing a snack or coloring, I'll ask Amelia some questions about how school is going, and then throw in a hypothetical, like "Hey, Smalls, what would you say if someone teased you about your whale shirt / tennis shoes / mismatched socks?" This gives her the opportunity to practice some comebacks like, "That's too bad you don't like my shirt. It's my total fave." Or "Everyone has different styles, it's what makes us full of awesome!" Even a simple "OK, thanks anyway" seems to dissipate the ire without Amelia having to be mean back or involve the teacher. This also gets us in the habit of having bunches of little talks as a way to check in with each other, something that I hope continues through high school and beyond.

In the Pigtail Pals community, parents frequently complain that their kids are being teased for the color of something they are wearing, or being the wrong gender for a character or hobby they really like. Kids pick up on the gender roles quickly and they are known to police others. Prepping your girl with some one-liners can help her slide through a situation if it arises:

"Colors are for everyone."

"I'm a girl and I'm wearing these shoes. They aren't boy shoes, they are kid shoes."

"If I like Buzz Lightyear / football / *Star Wars*, then it isn't just for boys, it is for me too."

"I'm just fine with the things I like."

"You don't need to tease me just because I am different from you."

Of course, not just kids but other parents can fail to be as accepting as they should be. I've heard of situations in which the kids are totally game for whatever, but the parents' closed minds create the problems. In that case, you can always deliver grown-up versions of the kids' comebacks above:

"I don't think it matters what colors the kids wear. They all seem content to me."

"We really enjoy that Amelia's interests are varied. What kinds of things interest your daughter?"

"I'm not really big on labeling things 'boys' or 'girls.' It doesn't seem like that big of a deal. I would rather just give them the space to be kids. They grow up so fast, right?"

"I find it a little inappropriate for an adult to be teasing a child. I treat your daughter with respect, and I ask that you extend that same courtesy to mine."

The other side to the coin of building up resiliency in Amelia is teaching her to be kind and accepting of others. We were walking to school one morning and farther ahead on the sidewalk an older boy had a neon pink backpack. Amelia commented he shouldn't have pink, it was a "girl's color." I reminded her that "colors are for everyone" and pointed out that she had a blue backpack. She then backtracked a bit and explained that she was only saying that because she didn't want him to get teased by other kids, not because she thought he shouldn't have pink. I suggested a better way to express that would be to tell the boy that she liked his bag and thought it was cool. If other students saw their peers being accepting of it, they might be less likely to tease him.

Carrie Goldman's book *Bullied: What Every Parent, Teacher, and Kid Needs to Know About Ending the Cycle of Fear* is a great resource that points out that the causes of bullying often revolve around some aspect of gender: gendered marketing and stereotypes, sexualization, body image, geek girls and princess boys, LGBTQ kids, and so on. It offers many great tips for kids to get past teasing, taunting, and bullying.

Letters from the Experts

Carrie Goldman

Carrie Goldman is a parent-activist and the author of *Bullied: What Every Parent, Teacher, and Kid Needs to Know About Ending the Cycle of Fear*. She blogs at www.chicagonow.com/portrait-of-an-adoption.

Dear Readers,

In November of 2010, my first-grade daughter, Katie, became upset because the boys at school were taunting her for carrying a *Star Wars* water bottle. They told her that *Star Wars* was "only for boys, not for girls," and they followed her around at lunch and at recess, making fun of her. Katie wanted the taunting to stop, so she decided to trade in her *Star Wars* water bottle for a butterfly water bottle. I wrote a post about it for my blog, *Portrait of an Adoption*. It was the post that launched a thousand geeks, as one of my readers joked.

There was an outpouring of support for Katie that came from people across the world. Thousands of men and women wanted to share their own stories about how they had been taunted and teased for similar reasons. Our family noticed a common theme in the responses—many of the people who had been bullied were targeted because they refused to conform to gender expectations. We heard from girls and women who were harassed for stepping outside of the realm of girly, pink princess–themed items. We heard from boys and men who suffered because they preferred dolls and dresses to sports and scruff.

Katie's story struck such a responsive chord that I decided to embark on a journey of researching and writing about bullying in our culture, with a heavy emphasis on analyzing the gendered world in which we live. There are layers of complexity to bullying. Those who engage in bullying do so for two main reasons: 1) They are lacking in empathy, and 2) They have a sense of entitlement that allows them to make value judgments about others based on stereotypes. Bullying is rooted in the fear and dislike of those who are different, and those fears are fostered by the practices of sexualization, misogyny, and homophobia.

As parents of three young daughters, my husband and I are working to chip away at society's negative messages directed at both females and males. There are all different ways to be a girl, and there are all different ways to be a boy. My husband Andrew encounters comments and stereotypes in the high school classes where he teaches, and he stops to address these bullying incidences as they occur. I write about the subtle (and not-so-subtle) ways that our children are influenced by the media, the Internet, the fashion industry, and celebrity culture.

Awareness of the issues is the first step. Once we began pointing out to our kids that goods and services are marketed with a gendered slant, they became savvier in their choices. We are trying to teach our daughters to question the messages the world thrusts at them, instead of accepting everything they are told. After awareness comes practice. Both kids and adults need practice at finding effective ways to respond to the world, especially if they are going to challenge established norms.

Through education, practice, and respectful communication, our kids have the power to redefine the social norms that contribute to bullying and prejudice. It is not easy, but it makes a difference, and even incremental change can have a lasting, positive effect. There are so many parents out there who are trying to leave the world a bit better for their children.

In support,
Carrie Goldman

But when I read up about raising successful students, bullying, leadership, and other topics around having a kid in school, I rarely come across information about what to do when it is the *teachers* reinforcing gender bias or stereotypes. Certainly it happens, as I hear about it all the time from parents within my social media community. I've been asked for advice on how to handle situations like: teachers teasing children about having a boyfriend or girlfriend, teachers reinforcing gender color-coding or stereotypes in the classroom, sexualized toys in the classroom, teachers not promoting cross-gender friendships, not stopping gender-based bullying, and taking away a toy or book and replacing it with something the teacher deems more appropriate for the child's gender.

As strange as these situations may sound, they are all real-world examples. They can be difficult for parents to navigate, as they have respect for the teachers and want to maintain an amicable relationship between their family and the school, while at the same time knowing there is no place for gender bias and stereotypes in the classroom. Lori Day, an educational psychologist, consultant, and the author of *Her Next Chapter,* says, "Teachers enjoy a uniquely powerful position of both authority and inspiration in a child's life. Given this dynamic, teachers can set a positive example in their classrooms by not replicating the gender stereotypes that are so ubiquitous in society at large. When teachers segregate their classrooms into the princess dress-up area for girls and the trucks and LEGO space for boys, this sends both girls and boys a very clear message about where and how they are expected to play and encourages the children themselves to police each other's play along gender lines."

Day also echoes the research of the Sanford Harmony Program, stating, "Classrooms that foster 'girl play' and 'boy play' also discourage cross-gender play, which is crucial at this age. When teachers reflexively categorize children by gender or inadvertently reinforce the differences between boys and girls instead of their commonalities— 'Boys, be quiet and sit down!' or 'Girls, let's tiptoe like fairies to the drinking fountain'—these messages are absorbed by children in ways that affect how they view themselves and each other and that undermine their otherwise limitless imaginations and aspirations."

However, she says, "when teachers take care to create a learning environment that allows all children to express who they are, without artificial gender boundaries, girls and boys flourish. Teachers have a singular role in the gender socialization of their students and need to be aware of this special clout in the eyes of doting children."

Parents can and should be active participants in their child's education. Most classrooms allow for observation, and if nothing else eating lunch with your student will help you get to know the school and the atmosphere. Volunteering for the parent-teacher organization is another great way to become hands-on with the school and develop a rapport with the staff. Keep an open dialogue with your child about how her school day went, how playtime with friends went, asking if anything happy or unhappy happened during the day, and so on.

Should your child share with you or should you overhear something about gender bias or stereotyping going on during the school day or sexualized toys in the classroom, Lori Day suggests this course of action:

1. Write downs notes from the incident, and follow-up questions you would like answered.
2. E-mail or phone the teacher to set up a face-to-face meeting. Express to the teacher that you are looking for a respectful and collaborative approach to a concern you have.
3. Organize your thoughts in advance of the meeting, and even print off articles or blog posts for the teacher to do further reading. Have one or two solutions to suggest, or have a couple of "asks," or things you would like to see change for the better for all students involved. An "ask" might be the teacher encouraging more boy-girl cooperative activities, or not grouping the class by boy / girl when lining up.
4. Parents can ask if they may contribute in any way, such as by offering volunteer time to help the teacher rearrange classroom toys or furniture, or by offering to donate toys that are not sexualized or promoting of stereotypes.

Day says, "Most teachers appreciate having a strong partnership with the parents of their students, so parents should not hesitate to politely let teachers know the ways in which they hope to partner around their child's school experience."

Teachers are such a huge part of our children's lives. I can remember every teacher I've ever had, and I still hold a special place in my heart for many of them. Teachers inspire, lift up, and propel our children forward. Let's give teachers all the support we can and act as partners in creating the healthiest learning environment for our children, both boys and girls. Offer resources, direct teachers to the Pigtail Pals social media sites and blog or any of the other great experts and resources in this book, and make sure your local library carries copies of the books listed in our Resources section so that your teachers can have access to the best learning materials.

Below is a sample letter that you can circulate among like-minded parents, who may sign on if they wish. You might want to present the letter to the teacher personally and in as positive and uplifting a manner as possible so he or she does not feel defensive. This letter could easily be adapted for the school principal or special-classes teacher such as the gym, art, or music teacher, if appropriate.

Dear _____,

We parents know how hugely important you will be to our children. We ask that you provide a classroom that is a vibrant and colorful learning space, free of commercialization, gender stereotypes, and sexualized media and toys.

As we're sure you are well aware, girls are currently stereotyped from birth and sexualized at ever-younger ages. Visit any infant layette section of a store, and you'll come across a sea of pink, and nothing but pink. As our girls grow, they receive unhealthy, limiting messages during their toddler and preschool years from media, clothing, and toys. For girls, the marketplace seems to focus on beauty, shopping, princess obsession, hyperfemininity, and sex appeal at too early an age.

At such a crucial time of development, we parents want to make sure these messages are not reinforced in the classroom. To that end, we respectfully make the following requests:

- We would like instruction in media literacy to begin in preschool and continue through the school years. It will take all of us working together to create change.
- We ask that our kids' classrooms stay commercial-free.
- Please ensure the toys, books, images, magazines, and websites used in your classroom represent girls as being smart, adventurous, kind, creative, and curious. It is also important for boys to see girls represented in a positive manner.
- We request that toys and media in our kids' learning environment be free of violence, sexual stereotypes, and sexual content.
- Please do not make art projects or lesson plans gender-specific. In place of a princess and knights–themed week, how about a fairy-tale unit, and teach stories from around the world with less focus on gender? Or, during art, let the boys and girls decide for themselves who wants to make a sword and who wants to make a magic wand.

We know as teachers that you value childhood as much as we do. Please ensure your classroom remains a tribute to childhood and the natural curiosity that resides there.

Thank you for making your classroom an amazing place for our kids to learn!

Sincerely,

[parent names]

Letters from the Experts

Jennifer Hartstein

Jennifer Hartstein is a child, adolescent, and family psychologist who lives and works in New York City. She's a contributor to many morning and news programs and the author of *Princess Recovery: A How-to Guide to Raising Strong, Empowered Girls Who Can Create Their Own Happily Ever Afters.*

Dear Parents,

So very often, in environments outside of your own, gender stereotypes are played out again and again. This issue is frequently most noticeable in places you would hope it would not be: schools or doctors' offices. Children are asked to line up boys on one side, girls on the other. Doctors offer pink for girls, blue for boys. The toys offered out of the treasure chest at the dentist are gender specific, and, if your child asks for something that is perceived to be "out of the norm," she may be questioned or made to feel "less than." We all want our daughters to grow up feeling as if they can take on anything, so it is your responsibility as the parent to model how to stand up for yourself, and show your daughter that she can too.

Parents do not always feel that it is their "right" to ask for changes when it comes to gender neutrality. A fear persists, especially in these environments, that the child will suffer, and bear the brunt of others' frustrations or lack of understanding, if the parent asks for alternatives. Although this fear is understandable, it has to be managed and worked through, especially if it is in the best interest of your daughter or son. You have the ability, as your child's advocate, to ask for what you want, and, subsequently, to teach your child to ask for what she wants.

It's scary to go against the norm. Isn't that true for everyone? Unfortunately, the norm can keep us stuck in patterns that might not be best for everyone, and that might actually teach our girls that they do not deserve the same things as the boys. We are seeing time and again how this message is perpetuated. Clearly, you see that too, as you want to redefine girly! In order to do it, you have to find your voice in the schools and with your doctor, and use it.

You may know it needs to be done, but don't know where to start. The first step is to take a deep breath and decide what you want to see happen. What change do you want to see within these systems that promotes success, determination, and confidence amongst the girls and boys there? Figure out what you want to say, and start to say it. You may have to repeat your message often in order to be heard. Don't give up! The second people start to listen, you have begun to initiate change. Change is scary. People don't like it. And, it has to happen. The more you teach those around you, and the more your child sees you doing so, the more encouraged she will be to do so for herself.

Making sure your voice is heard may be a new experience for you, as well. Doesn't it feel empowering? Pass on that empowerment to your daughter. The world will be a better place with more empowered girls (and boys), who can continue to redefine girly.

You've got this, and you'll be great. And your daughter? She'll be *amazing*.

Warmly,
Jennifer Hartstein

Shopping Strategies—
Saying No to Sexed-Up Clothes
and Yes to a Personal Brand

In part because I was selective about what media I allowed during her preschool years and in part because of her personality, Amelia isn't much into fashion, trends, or brands. We focus on clothes that allow her to play hard, so in the summertime she's in tank tops and cotton shorts and in the cooler months she likes leggings and long-sleeved T-shirts, or knit tights under T-shirt dresses. Right now it feels like any arguments over wearing an inappropriate or revealing outfit will be years away. We'll see how that works out for me.

But ask parents what happens when their girls outgrow size 5T or 6T, and you get the dreaded response, "We have to shop in the big girls' department." Gone, for the most part, are the cute comfortable play clothes and one-piece tank swimsuits as we now navigate the racks of clothing and swimwear choices that turn young girls into mini-adults, complete with touches of overt sexiness. I want my eight-year-old to dress like an eight-year-old, not an eighteen- or twenty-eight-year-old.

For parents with children under the age of about ten, this is nothing new. Hip-hugger jeans, string bikinis, padded bras, and heeled shoes—all in child sizes—have been available now for well over a decade. Some marketers call this the Britney Effect, referring to pop star Britney Spears's emergence on the scene in the late 1990s.

In the age of KGOY (kids getting older younger) and brand awareness developing in kids at age two to three, marketers know from meticulous research that kids have an ever-increasing influence on how parents spend dollars. Licensed characters and celebrities appear on nearly every child product in the big box shops. The power of the "nag factor" (the tendency of children bombarded with marketing to unrelentingly request advertised items) is huge, plus the pressure to be "cool" and "popular" (usually defined as "sexy" and "grown-up"), can make it difficult for parents to stand their ground and make decisions that are best for the child. Age compression has resulted in sexy pop stars and teen magazines being coveted not just by fifteen-year-olds but by nine-year-olds. Yet there is a huge difference between the development of a fourth-grader and that of a sophomore in high school. More than ever, childhood no longer looks like childhood.

Kids have always wanted to be regarded as older than they are; that is nothing new. What is new is that now marketers are free to advertise that concept directly to children, and they seem to lack the scruples to understand that our highly sexualized raunch culture and adult sexuality really have no place in childhood, nor are they an appropriate way to seduce young consumers.

To be fair, I do not think all marketers are evil. I know women who are marketers and recognize the same problems in marketing that the Pigtail Pals community does. One of the most successful advertising executives of our time, Alex Bogusky, left the business in part because he felt strongly about not advertising to children.

But there is huge money to be made through cradle-to-grave marketing, and the sooner corporations can get kids buying and spending like adults, the quicker they meet their bottom lines and the happier their shareholders will be. Besides, they reason, if parents don't like it, they can just not buy it, right?

Wrong. It is too easy to blame the parents, says Sharon Lamb, coauthor of *Packaging Girlhood*. "Blaming the parents is exactly what the marketers want you to do. They spend $12 billion getting your kids to want the things you don't want them to have, and then they blame you for buying them."

We aren't talking about one or two stores offering some distasteful items. We are talking about a cultural shift in how companies are designing and making goods for children. Our sex-saturated culture has trickled down into childhood, comfortably settling in girlhood, specifically. While there are positive choices out there, they are usually three to four times as expensive and only available through specialty shops or catalogs. Research shows that nearly 30 percent of girls' clothing (sizes toddler to preteen) offered at popular retailers is sexualized, while overall 86 percent of girls' clothing carries a combination of both childlike and sexy characteristics. If ever two words did not belong together, it is "childlike" and "sexy."

When did things change so drastically? In the mid-1990s the deregulation of children's advertising was a decade old. Music executives were trying to revitalize the money machine that is teen pop stars after the early-90s grunge / Riot Grrrl wave, and the Internet was coming of age, making porn available 24/7. I was in college when the crop of overly-sexualized teen stars hit the scene in the late 1990s. Britney Spears, Christina Aguilera, and the more mature Spice Girls and Pussycat Dolls were all the rage, and my friends and I could not make sense of it. Collectively these acts were being marketed as "girl power," but they looked a lot like soft-core porn to us. If that was girl power, it was a very co-opted sense of the word. It felt more like commercialized sexual objectification through the male gaze. We were seeing the little girls we babysat being introduced to some very adult concepts as the sexy singers ushered in even sexier dolls and clothes. Hot pants and a bare tummy on a doll is disturbing enough; a child dressed the same way is even more so.

But parents are the ones buying all this, right? Kids don't have money. Why would a parent want his or her little girl to play at being sexy and think it was cute? Further, why is it OK for a prepubescent girl to play at sexy, but a teen girl gets slut-shamed for expressing and experimenting with her sexuality?

In *So Sexy So Soon: The New Sexualized Childhood and What Parents Can Do to Protect Their Kids*, Diane E. Levin and Jean Kilbourne discuss the double bind that teenage girls are in these days. Simply put, our girls are expected to be sexy virgins—to look hot and available at all times but not actually engage in sex lest they be given a scarlet letter. Sex through the male gaze is all around these girls and they are growing up in a culture in which celebrities like Paris Hilton and Kim Kardashian gained fame from releasing sex tapes (despite having no apparent talents). Add to that, the desired look and beauty regimen expected of girls today come right off the pages of the pornography industry playbook.

Of course, girls have always pretended to be older or tried on makeup or certain fashions, but these were only temporary visits to the Land of Grown-Up. By the late 1990s, makeup, heels, sexy clothing, sexy dolls, and sexy teen stars were being marketed directly to children. Susan Linn, the cofounder of the Campaign for a Commercial-Free Childhood, describes this as the "ratcheting up of the kind of precocious, irresponsible sexuality that is being marketed to little girls." So how do parents keep the Britney Effect at bay and preserve childhood just a little bit longer?

First, we need to be educated consumers. And we need to have a game plan for when we are shopping:

1. Get your parenting partner on board with the commitment to not purchase sexualized items. Be aware of stores and brands to watch out for.
2. Be committed to not giving in to whining/begging in the store, and have preset responses, rules, and consequences around that behavior. For little ones, say something like, "Olivia, you know that whining stops conversation and gets an automatic no" or for older girls, "Your whining is not helping us decide if this is

appropriate for you, so we'll have to look at it another time when we are ready to make good decisions" and then move to a different part of the store. Or, "All of your friends wearing this does not influence my decision. Having your best interest at heart is what guides my decisions and my answer is still a no." Like my mom used to say, "I'm not saying no, I'm saying, 'I love you' in a way you'll understand years later."

3. Have some guidelines to follow to determine whether an item is a fit for your family or not:

   ❋ Does the item try to make someone very little appear very grown-up?

   ❋ Does the item allow her to move and play the way a child her age should?

   ❋ Does the item send messages that are sexual and age-inappropriate?

   ❋ Does the item align with your family values and your daughter's personality?

   ❋ Does the item convey messages that show respect for her as a whole person?

4. Pretend you have to write a blog post about this purchase a month from now. Would you stand by the decision you are about to make? Or would you regret it or have to rationalize it? If it is a questionable choice, are you ready to turn it into a teachable moment? Does the item align with the values you are teaching your kids on a daily basis?

5. Involve your children in the decision-making process (with the parent having the final say) so that they learn and understand how to think critically about what messages are being marketed to them, and what it says about them as a consumer of these messages.

Whether the object in question is a swimsuit or an outfit or an impractical pair of shoes, we want to try not to say the item is "inappropriate" or "bad" but rather "not appropriate for your age" or "the message it sends is too grown-up for a girl your age."

A short skirt or revealing bikini or high heels are fine for an adult woman, but not for a little girl. Sexuality is a great thing, when it is on your own terms. Women need the freedom to express their sexuality without being labeled or shamed for it, and girls need the freedom to come into this age on their own terms. Sexy is great; sexualization is unhealthy.

To get your child involved and on board with making healthy decisions for herself, try the discussion openers below. You'll notice some of them are similar to the list of responses when talking about toys from chapter 5; they cross over nicely when talking about clothes, shoes, or swimsuits that are sexy beyond your daughter's years.

"This dress/bikini/shirt looks a little too grown-up for you. I'd like to help you find something similar, but more appropriate for a girl your age."

"I understand why you like this and think it's cool, but this shows off too much of your body. We want people to notice you because you are an awesome person, not because your bottom is hanging out."

"Do you think that outfit will pass the dress code at school? Why do you think school has a dress code?"

"I'm thinking that while you feel that bikini looks cool, I think it looks like something a grown woman would wear to be sexy. Sexy isn't something a girl your age should be concerned about."

"That outfit makes you look so much like a grown-up, I think it is meant for much older girls. Maybe it is something we can consider in a few years."

"I think it is unnecessary to expose your cleavage like that. Do you understand the message an outfit like that gives, when you display your breasts like that? What kind of attention do you think that might bring?"

"I think you might have a hard time doing fun things in those sorts of clothes/shoes. It might be hard to run and jump and really use your body for playing. In our family we know bodies are for being active and having adventures, so let's find an outfit/pair of non-heeled shoes that can do all the great things you like to do."

"What do you like about that shirt/skirt/dress/pair of shoes?" Listen to the answers. Try to find a compromise.

You need to decide what is acceptable or not for your family and then teach the "why" of that to your children. "No, because I said so," doesn't do a lot of teaching, and it doesn't really respect the child or her ability to think. Parents do need to set limits and say no, but how we do it will make the difference in raising little consumers who are tuned in rather than blindly following the marketing. Our end game in this is raising children who hear our voices and see our faces when they face the hard decisions in life. Helping them now to sort through conflicting messages and desires will enable them down the road to make the right call when the stakes are higher and the problems are bigger.

Your Daughter's Personal Brand

One of the ways parents can get their daughters to think critically about marketing and to feel comfortable rejecting "what everyone else" is wearing or doing is to help her develop a personal brand. By this I mean a trademark identity and personality that she leaves like a business card for the world to see. Marketers will try to brand her from day one, but I say let her define herself. By having a personal brand she has an understanding of who she is, the values of the family she comes from, and where she wants to take herself in this world. It means that success and achievement come from self-definition and self-packaging. It means authenticity, transparency, knowing your goals, adding value to your community, and creating a footprint.

Your daughter can define for herself who she will be in this world, with guidance from her family, teachers, positive peers, and mentors as sources of encouragement that help her to become a remarkable young adult. You want her to make the right decisions not because she is following someone's rules or limitations for her but rather because she has a solid understanding of her own values and what syncs with those values and what doesn't.

I remember the moment I knew what I wanted my "brand" to be. I wasn't thinking about it in those terms at the time, but it was the moment I remember thinking, "This is what I want to be like as a grown-up" and feeling like I had the road map to get me there. I was an eighth-grader at a student council conference and the keynote speaker told a story about his high school reunion and the table he sat at among his old friends. Actually, he described two types of tables. Table A spent the night talking about all the amazing and crazy things they had done together. Table B's conversation was a recollection of watching Table A do it all. The speaker then asked which table we would want to be sitting at twenty years from now. He went on to tell us the decisions we make hold meaning, and how to make decisions that bring us closer to the person we want to be.

In that moment, my brand was born. I wanted to be a Table A person. I wanted to be a leader and a change maker. I wanted all of those awesome and fun memories to be my own, not memories of watching someone else do it all. I consciously started making decisions and taking actions that brought me closer to that goal. I knew what I wanted my long-term brand to be, and I recognized situations or relationships that conflicted with that.

Here are some things for you and your daughter to think about as you assist her in creating her personal brand:

❋ What kind of visual presentation does your daughter give? Does her manner of dress ask people to focus on her as a whole person, or as a collection of sexual body parts? Does she hold her head up and look people in the eye? Does she speak clearly and articulate? Does she know how to give a proper handshake and stand on her feet with confidence? These are the kinds of things that will influence teachers, scholarship boards, college admissions counselors, mentors, and job interviewers.

❋ What about the overall state of her communications? Does she have a supportive and dedicated group of friends? Is she a leader or does she let someone else carve a path for her to follow? Does she repeat the "fat talk" she hears? Does she respect her body and treat herself in a healthy and caring way? Does she add value to her community? Is she creating her own footprint? How you communicate to your daughter, how she communicates with herself, and how she interacts with her world at young ages will determine how confidently she enters adolescence and adulthood.

❋ What about her credo and ethics? What kind of mission statement would she craft for herself? What is her passion and how does she honor that? Does she conduct herself in a way that shows respect both for herself and for your family values and rules? Does she admit when she is wrong and take ownership of her mistakes? Oftentimes life isn't about being the smartest or prettiest person in the room, it is about being the most authentic. Authenticity is like a muscle that needs constant strengthening and conditioning—your daughter needs to be taught to be faithful to herself. Always.

I talk about a personal brand during my workshops, and one time a parent asked me when we should start teaching this. The answer, of course, is right away. Whether your daughter is two or twelve years old, she is ready to think about her sense of self. I use the example from the book and movie *The Help*. In that story we are introduced to the mighty Aibileen Clark, an African American maid working in the 1960s south. Every day she tells her little charge, toddler Mae Mobley, "You is smart. You is kind. You is important." That is the very beginning of helping your daughter to build a brand.

A personal brand will shift and reshape over time, but the core values remain. I am not the same person I was at fifteen or twenty-five. My personal brand has adjusted as life has taught me new and different lessons, but my understanding of who I am has remained the same. A five-year-old does not need to have her whole life planned out, but she does need a sense of who she is as she explores, learns, creates, makes mistakes, and succeeds along the way.

One definition of "brand" reads: "The recognition and perception of a brand is highly influenced by its visual presentation. A brand's visual identity is the overall look of its communications." As my daughter grows I will teach her that she should not judge people by their manner of dress but that, at the same time, the clothes we wear send a message about how we feel about ourselves and what we want others to think about us. They are our "visual presentation." Girls who "put it all on display" seem to give the impression they are little more than a collection of sexual body parts. We can teach (and show) our girls how to present themselves as a whole person. As adults, we know that true sexiness is most powerful when we leave the details to the imagination. I would argue a nine- or fourteen-year-old girl should have prerogatives other than looking sexy. As the adults responsible for shaping these girls, we need to leave pejoratives out of the conversation. *Tramp, slut, whore, hoochie, bimbo, floozy, tart, future stripper,* and *hussy* are judgments, not descriptions, of girls. Those words say more about the person using them than they do the girl they are aimed at.

The tween and teen years are a perfect time for girls to experiment with styles and discover what they are comfortable wearing as their personal brand changes and matures, and we need to afford our daughters the space to make some mistakes. One blue hair dye or low-cut shirt or miniskirt does not undo a girl, but the judgment and harsh comments they elicit can. One negative comment can undo a thousand compliments. We can teach our girls to give thought to what they wear while not tearing down other girls for their decisions. It can be a fine line to walk.

Dressing "so sexy so soon" at school and in social situations can provoke some righteous girl hate, but it also impacts friendships with the opposite sex. Explains Crystal Smith, author of *The Achilles Effect: What Pop Culture Is Teaching Boys About Masculinity*, "When a girl dresses in a provocative manner, she is unwittingly reinforcing what boys see in the pop culture that surrounds them. . . . This is not to say that the girl is 'asking for it.' She may simply be acting out what she sees in magazines, TV programs, and films, without even understanding it. But boys, who see the same kinds of sexualized images as girls, may believe that she is asking for the kind of attention that her clothes suggest she wants and react accordingly."

Women are widely shown as objects of the male gaze in the media, and this contributes to girls adopting this attitude and objectifying themselves, advertising their sexuality at ages before they truly understand the messages they are sending. This cycle has to stop, and helping your daughter develop an alternate brand for herself that flies in the face of a stereotyping and sexualizing culture is one place to start.

Letters from the Experts

Amy Jussel

Amy Jussel is founder and executive director of Shaping Youth, a nonprofit consortium using the power of media for positive change.

❋ ❋ ❋

Dear Parents,

It's a given that parenting values will be challenged by a hyper-sexualized marketplace for kids, which Senator Tom Harkin described as "throwing acid on their innocence." Armed with a critical thinking shield and a persuasive parenting saber, there's an opportunity to thrive, not just survive, in the battle for kids' hearts and minds to change the channel of influence!

Parents who are mindful of media messages and what we "buy into" gift their children with clarity. By "walking the walk" rather than lowering the bar in limbo mode to "excuse" a culture that rewards profit over public health, we're role modeling for kids how to draw clear boundaries, "use our voice" (in purchasing power AND peer dynamics), and stand and deliver.

How many times have you heard, "Lighten up, it's just a toy" or "It's a string bikini, it's not a thong. What's the big deal?" or "C'mon, she doesn't even understand what that means" (insert music lyrics, TV show, dance gyrations, or media of choice). It's particularly upending when an adult (spouse/family included) mocks your convictions with loaded words like "Don't be so judgmental" (or controlling, uptight, neurotic, overprotective, self-righteous) because you're being undermined from within your own safety zone. It can be disheartening, and maybe even make you doubt your own convictions when "group think" takes hold. Trust yourself.

Once we "see," it can't be unseen. Those "Aha" moments and life skills you're imparting will resurface and reprise like a comforting déjà vu for the child who can recognize and apply with confidence, "This feels familiar, yep, been down this road before, no problem, I can handle this."

As parents, we sometimes underestimate our own worth in the influence arena, feeling outgunned by marketing mortar fire lobbing grenades of "so sexy so soon" cues into our peaceful foxholes of home life. But as Albert Einstein said, "Setting an example is not the main means of influencing another, it is the *only* means."

Good luck,
Amy Jussel

Using Your Voice and Consumer Power to Fight the Companies Making Major Missteps

My social media community hears me say two little mantras quite a lot: "When we know better, we can do better" and "Be not silent." The first I learned after hearing my longtime shero Maya Angelou speak. The second was taught to me by a Holocaust survivor during my senior year of high school. It is these two ideals that drive me every day to use my voice, my blog, and my social media communities to create awareness and inspire change among parents.

Change in the marketplace and in the media are not going to happen overnight, but we can enact an immediate shift in our consumer and media habits and in how we communicate with companies. Not every actionable item I take on results in game-changing marketing practices or coverage in the press, but by the hundreds of e-mails and messages I get, I know the community around Pigtail Pals & Ballcap Buddies has changed the way parents shop, spend money, and parent their children. If I only had a dollar for every time I have received a message that begins, "I was out shopping and thought of you when . . . "

One of the first blog posts I ever wrote for the *Redefine Girly* blog was about a shopping trip with then–four-year-old Amelia for her first bicycle. Going on bike rides as a family while growing up in Wisconsin is a fond childhood memory of mine and I was quite excited about Amelia reaching this milestone. I was expecting the limited and stereotypical pink/purple/turquoise color choices. I was expecting sparkles and butterflies. I was expecting almost all of the choices to be character-branded with the Disney princess crew, Hannah Montana, Barbie, and the rest.

What I wasn't expecting was that even children's bicycles have become sexualized. Of all things, the quintessential part of childhood—a first bike—carries a sexualized message on it. Like the Huffy bike model, sized sixteen inches, displaying the words MAJOR FLIRT on it. This size bike is recommended for ages three to six years old. Is it really in the best interest of our children to send them freelancing around the neighborhood on a bike letting everyone know they are a flirtatious coquette? And, is Major Flirt as bad as Huffy's Hot Stuff model, also recommended for three- to six-year-old girls? Do three- to six-year-old girls have stuff that is hot? Should girls aged three to six be flirting?

Most kids ride their bikes outdoors and in public, where anybody can see them. So what happens to the little girl who is unfortunate enough to be alone and riding her "Hot Stuff" bike past a group of older boys who surround her and start questioning her on how hot her stuff really is? Can a six-year-old handle that kind of street harassment? Should she have to? A child at this age would probably lack the social skills and vocabulary necessary to stop sexual advances from a predator or older children. Why do I have to use the phrase "sexual advances" in a post about my daughter's first bike?

I went home and researched bike selections at the popular big box stores like Target, K-Mart, and Walmart. In the price range we were looking at for our daughter's first bike (less than $80), these were the model names from numerous manufacturers: So Sweet, Pop Star, Dream Journey, Spring Fling, Hot Stuff, Major Flirt, Daisy Diva, Sea Star, Twirl, Pizazz, Mist, DeeLite, Jasmine, Precious, and Candy. A quick search of the selection of Huffy girls' bikes in 2012 shows some improvement, as they have dropped the sexualized names, which is fantastic.

When I originally published this blog post I called Huffy Bike headquarters and had two very nice conversations with a marketing manager, a mother of two grown daughters. She told me she understood my concern, and said when Huffy came up with the names Hot Stuff and Major Flirt, they were influenced by fashion and what was popular in girls' clothing at the time. She went on to say how uncomfortable the sexy clothing trends had made her feel when she was raising her now-grown daughters. She informed me that due to "a number of calls from parents" about these names, Huffy was no longer manufacturing them. Because they were still carried in stores, I asked if Huffy provided stickers or anything that parents could use to cover up the words. She said no. (I created vinyl Pigtail Pals stickers to take care of this.) Although the bike models with sexualized names were still available at retailers and promoted on the Huffy website, she said Huffy was trying to be more sensitive to those kinds of things. I asked for a statement reflecting such and I got this:

> Huffy has been working to help parents and children with bicycling for years. We've never seen ourselves as just bike manufacturers. To us, it's more than that. Biking is a way for both adults and kids to be active outdoors. The Huffy website has a lot of information to help make sure bicycle riding is enjoyable and safe. Www.Huffy.com has tips for parents teaching their children how to ride a bike; bicycle safety posters for kids; guides for finding a bike path in your area; and much more.

Well, that's not really what I was looking for. I wanted a major corporation like Huffy to say something like *Huffy has been proudly making bikes for parents and children for years. We are more than just bike manufacturers. To us, biking is a way for families to enjoy the outdoors in a healthy and safe way. Connected to our commitment to safety is the knowledge that our bikes carry messages and images that allow for healthy and age-appropriate development. We responsibly consider all areas of your child's safety when developing, marketing, and promoting our cycling products.*

Via e-mail, I thanked the Huffy representative for her time, sent her my wording (above) for a statement that does a better job of taking ownership of the issue, offered alternative bike model names, and offered my time to consult with them should they want more information on this area of marketing, gender, and sexualization.

I don't know if any immediate battles were won in the war on sexualization with my actions and my post about Huffy, but the discussion that ensued on social media put the Pigtail Pals blog on the map and was a tipping point for a lot of parents following the story. "I see it now, and I see it everywhere" was a frequent comment from parents.

After the Huffy episode, my next project was taking the family-friendly store Kohl's to task after I found G-string panties being sold next to training bras in the Juniors department. I compared it to peanut butter and jelly being sold next to each other in the grocery store: they are stocked together because they go together. But do tweens buying their first bra also need to be wearing the skimpiest panties made for women?

The panties were from the brand Candie's, infamous for the Lolita-like, heavy-on-the-pink ad campaigns using young pop stars and actresses in seductive poses with the obligatory finger-by-the-mouth, "Oopsie, am I sexy?" look. Candie's seems to have a track record of taking young women and turning them into sultry, sexy spokesmodels for a clothing line that actually isn't that racy or sexy. But sex sells, and in the age of KGOY, Candie's markets to a young teen demographic eager to prove how grown-up they are.

I reached both Kohl's and Candie's for comments on my blog post. Kohl's told me that I could vote with my money and not buy it. The customer service manager told me, and I quote, "Bottom line, it sells." That's right, the sexualization of their tween and teen customers helps them meet their bottom line.

When you shop at Kohl's, the racy Candie's ads aren't there (they save those for the teen magazines) because the store puts up more wholesome marketing photos for mom to see. When I challenged Candie's about marketing sexy panties to young girls, a rep from Candie's left a comment on my blog, then sent me a message on Twitter, then sent me an e-mail, all with contradictory or absent contact information and three different age ranges they were purportedly targeting. First it was sixteen to twenty-one years old. But their own website says seven to sixteen and juniors. Then an e-mail response said eighteen to twenty-four years old.

I never was able to get a concise answer from Candie's, but what I do know is that I put the G-string on the small mannequin that I use for displaying my business's children's T-shirts, and it fit perfectly on a child's size 6–8 mannequin. I had no problem fitting the thong onto the form that has a twenty-nine-inch hip measurement (US standard hip measurement for a ten-year-old girl is twenty-eight and a half inches).

Putting aside that there are some very petite adult women out there who have every right to wear this kind of underwear if they so choose, why is a family department store stocking highly sexualized underwear in the juniors department? We know that young teens and tweens are the ones shopping here. Does a fifth-grader need a thong?

The tiniest of thongs is called a G-string. Female strippers and exotic dancers have referred to the style of thongs they wear for their performances as G-strings since the mid-1920s. I decided to ask a stripper what she thought of Candie's G-strings being marketed to tween and teen girls and the overall sexualization of girls' products. I called the "house mom," Amber, at a local strip club, and she said, "People may not agree with what I do for a living, but I pay my bills and provide for my family, and people coming in the club to see the shows are legal, eighteen and over. But in the stores, that isn't the case. Girls can buy those thongs but they wouldn't be allowed to even peek into the club if they were under eighteen. My industry gets criticized a lot, but we don't take advantage of kids; we don't make money off of kids like those corporations do."

I blogged about my conversations with Kohl's, Candie's, and Amber and e-mailed a copy of the text to Kohl's and Candie's. I received no further comment from Kohl's or Candie's, but the blog post had over twenty-seven thousand views and in the comments section many people pledged to contact Kohl's and Candie's and cancel their Kohl's credit cards.

While I do think Amber's industry (erotic dancing) plays a role in sexualization and the marketing of raunch culture to kids, I also think she is correct that the individual strip clubs aren't making money off kids the same way companies who make sexy juniors clothes and children's toys do. In fact, the tween market (eight- to twelve-year-olds) in the United States is estimated to wield $43 billion in spending power every year. Those are some major dollars coming into the companies we are hoping to convince to change the way they do business. Yes, it is an uphill climb.

What can families who see problems with gendered or sexualized products in the children's marketplace do to create change?

- ❀ Parents can vote with their dollars and not buy gendered or sexualized products. Retail can both prompt and respond to consumer demand.
- ❀ Parents (and kids) can communicate with retailers and manufacturers about why they are not buying certain products. This can be done directly in the store with a manager or by contacting the consumer relations department of that company via phone, e-mail, or letter.
- ❀ Parents can use social media (blogs, Twitter, Facebook, YouTube or Vimeo, Tumblr) to further the reach of their consumer voice and aggregate with other like-minded people. You never know how far you can go—several of my blog posts have been featured as stories on CNN's *Headline News*, FOX *News*, *Ms.* magazine, and a number of local news outlets.
- ❀ Parents can petition or protest companies with letters, e-mails, and online petition sites such as www.change.org or www.Care2.com.

❋ Parents can approach local television stations and newspapers, magazine editors, and producers at national television news-magazines with concerns or a specific story.

As a mom and an advocate, I have done all of the above. I am a thoughtful and responsible consumer; I talk to store managers regularly (with positive and negative comments); I use several forms of social media daily to express my views; I have helped to create and have signed many online petitions; and I have been featured in both local and national press working as an advocate against sexualization and gender stereotypes in children's products. I have also consulted with companies on products when they have asked how to be more mindful of sexualization, and I have lobbied for healthy media for youth on Capitol Hill.

During the fall of 2011 there was a trio of events in which consumer activists spoke out and companies buckled, and all of it took place over social media. It was incredible to be a part of and watch it happen. Even more incredible was that these stories gained major press in some of the biggest news outlets in the country.

The series began when JCPenney pulled their I'M TOO PRETTY TO DO HOMEWORK SO MY BROTHER DOES IT FOR ME T-shirt off their website in September 2011 after a social media firestorm that began with a tweet and Facebook status update by Pigtail Pals. Late one evening I called out JCPenney for the awful T-shirt on my social media sites and then e-mailed one of my artists to create a T-shirt for a counter-campaign with the message PRETTY'S GOT NOTHING TO DO WITH IT that we would launch the next day. Then I went to bed, because my daughter had her first day of kindergarten in the morning and it was a big day for our family.

When I woke the next morning, a Change.org petition had been launched by two young women in New York City that had gained thousands of signatures overnight, reporters were e-mailing and calling me, a front-page article on Yahoo! Shine was written about me, and by noon that next day JCPenney had pulled the shirt and issued a statement addressing the situation. When I launched the challenging

T-shirt that afternoon I watched hundreds of orders come in. Thanks to the power of social media and some national press, my little business went viral and I had the opportunity to sell empowering T-shirts to families all over the world.

ChapStick caused another social media firestorm and takedown that happened at rapid speed. The company had launched an ad that prominently featured a woman's backside up in the air while she straddled a couch. The premise was that she was looking for her lost Chap-Stick and loyal ChapStick users would identify with her plight. It was a move that blew up in ChapStick's face, as feminist media literacy blogger Margot Magowan of Reel Girl immediately sent out a call for action after a guest post on her blog by Melissa Spiers, encouraging her readers to sign the Change.org petition to have ChapStick cease the ad campaign immediately and to comment on the ChapStick Facebook page. Pigtail Pals quickly joined the cause, and then watched as dozens of our followers' comments were deleted from the ChapStick Facebook page. The heat from Facebook, Twitter, and the blogosphere became so hot that ChapStick did call for a stop to that ad campaign, and then issued one of the worst corporate apologies ever. (The apology itself made news in *Forbes*.)

There have been other gains in speaking out against corporations through online protest. Through a group effort by Pigtail Pals and my sister organizations and activists SPARK, Hardy Girls Healthy Women, Powered by Girl, Reel Girl, Peggy Orenstein, Margot Magowan, Princess Free Zone, and Jennifer Shewmaker's Operation Transformation we launched a blogging and Change.org campaign against the highly gendered LEGO Friends line. The online petition gained over fifty thousand signatures and resulted in LEGO inviting my colleagues from SPARK Movement to a sit-down at their corporate headquarters to discuss the new "girls" Friends line. With a face-to-face meeting the two sides were better able to communicate, and the SPARK delegates did a wonderful job expressing the parental and consumer concerns over this line.

Similarly, I have traveled to Mattel corporate headquarters to consult with the toy giant in an "influencer meeting" on their Monster

High line. I was a known adversary to the brand; nonetheless we had a constructive two-hour meeting that truly allowed for the girl advocates present to authentically communicate to the Monster High design and marketing teams. The meeting was friendly, common ground was reached, and I worked as a team with Whitney Smith of Girls for a Change to pitch several ideas that have the potential to create positive changes in the brand.

In these circumstances, with an entire product line like Monster High already in place, making millions of dollars in profit every quarter, and not easily removed (unlike a T-shirt design or ad campaign), it seemed more beneficial to arrange for a face-to-face meeting to explain the issue to a team from the company and work toward a solution. These influencer meetings at Mattel were created by independent consultant Jess Weiner, a noted author, speaker, and expert on self-esteem in girls and women. Weiner had been working with Mattel for nearly two years to create change from within, encouraging them to establish a pro-social arm to the Monster High brand, and has begun to effect change on the appearance and apparel of the dolls. Weiner's approach is to combine strategy, action, and community building by working from within a corporation. There has been success with this "inside influencer" approach, and it is one I stand by, though admittedly it is not available for great numbers of parents to directly participate in. Because of Weiner's careful and well-planned work with Mattel, I was invited in and was able to act as a representative for my parent community and bring all of my community's voices to the table.

Letters from the Experts

Jess Weiner

Jess Weiner is the owner of Talk to Jess, LLC. She uses story-telling for social change, specializing in helping brands cultivate positive media and marketing messages targeted toward women and girls. She is Dove's global ambassador for self-esteem and the author of *A Very Hungry Girl* and *Life Doesn't Begin Five Pounds from Now*.

❖ ❖ ❖

Dear Amazing Parent,

I know that if you are reading this letter (and this book) that you care very much about making the world a better place for your children. And part of making the world a better place is speaking out when you see something that blatantly stands in the way of achieving that goal.

But so many of us were raised to not use our voice to express displeasure, or question mainstream imagery, or demand a change. To do that meant we were being contrary or "difficult." And that's where I want to start—with those labels that keep us from speaking out. Let's dump them. And let's dump them for our children, too. Let's teach them to think critically, trust their gut instinct, and raise their voice when they are guided to.

And the same goes for you, dear parents. You also must dump the nagging voice that tells you that you "don't know what you are talking about" or that "no one will listen to you." That's the first step. Because as long as you are led by those internal voices or outdated family and social traditions, you will be standing in your own way.

Next, you have to figure out the best strategy necessary to make the change you desire. The formula to make change isn't a one-size-fits-all formula. Sometimes it requires a rage that is unrelenting. Sometimes it calls for an organized boycott or a sarcastic blog post. Sometimes it takes slow and steady pressure applied through e-mails, tweets, and in-person meet-ups. And sometimes it takes slow, steady strategy.

Teaching our children to be instruments of change is important, but we also have to teach our children that seeing a result from raising our voice could take some time. And in this "instaculture" we live in, anything that takes more than sixty seconds seems like an eternity. But teach them that the change they seek to make (whether it's challenging stereotypes about gender, or speaking up when the media sends hypersexualized messages to girls) is worth their fight. It's worth a steady application of energy and passion. It's worth a continued critical thinking about what they consume and how they *feel* when they consume that image.

As an expert in the area of women, girls, and media, I often work within large brands, businesses, and the media to help create authentic, empowering, diverse, and nuanced stories that reflect the reality of women's and girls' lives. My work is rooted in understanding that long-lasting social change is both fluid and consistent.

But this work isn't easy. And it's far from quick. I know firsthand that sometimes all it takes is one strong voice with a well-crafted letter to stop a campaign in its tracks. And I also have experienced the empty results of boycotts when what was needed instead was a humane, face-to-face meeting.

Sometimes in this fight for a more equitable media representation, you have to change directions, mix up strategy, and continue trying even in the face of inaction. It's also equally important to remember that the people making media are just that—people. Which means they are fallible and sometimes misguided and oftentimes willing to do the right thing when addressed as fellow human beings, with dignity and respect. And remember to claim the small victories. To hear the "yesses" and to be willing to change your own mind, too.

All of this ends up helping our children to become creative problem solvers, educated consumers, smart communicators, and unrelenting champions of social change. When we focus on encouraging these traits in our children, we will succeed in doing something no amount of media consumption can undo—we will have created compassionate, vibrant, and determined change makers who see raising their voices as not just something they do when they're angry but when they are dreaming of a bigger, better world for everyone.

Yours in Action,
Jess Weiner

The great thing about events like the JCPenney T-shirt-gate or the ChapStick implosion or the LEGO Friends blog riot was that parents were able to watch people enact change in real time. Coverage on these stories that began as grassroots actions by me and my colleagues went everywhere—CNN, *TODAY*, *Good Morning America*, *FOX News*, *New York Times*, *Forbes*, Jezebel, Yahoo! Shine, ABC's *20/20*, *Dateline NBC*, and the *Wall Street Journal*, to name a few. I received many messages after that firestorm period from parents saying they never would have spoken up about a product or advertising that bothered them, but now they saw the value in and need to do so.

Parents can take to social media to launch enormous protests and to let media content creators know they have crossed a line, as we saw happen in May 2013. Disney tried to give Merida, the fresh-faced

Scottish teen princess from "Brave," a sexy makeover for her official princess coronation. The public outcry went viral within days of the very adult, vixen looking Merida getting leaked, and the story was covered in mainstream media for weeks. Disney received so much pushback, they had to retract the redesign and return Merida to her healthy, girl-positive roots. My colleagues and I found this media event to be a tipping point, and we founded the Brave Girls Alliance (www .bravegirlswant.com) to function as a think tank and activist community where parents could join in the fight to protect girlhood from early sexualization by anxious marketers.

Also in May 2013, we saw thousands of parents use social media to tell a corporation about the media they want to see, like the fast and furious push to get the Female Minifigure Set on the LEGO CUUSOO website to the 10,000 votes necessary for the project to be considered for production. After the set reached the 10,000 votes needed, I then launched a Change.org petition asking LEGO to consider making this set and explaining why gender balance in the world's second-largest toy line was important. The petition letter, signed by more than 40,000 individuals, tells LEGO that parents and consumers would like to see the proposed set of female scientists and adventurers go into production and available for retail sale.

Here are some best practices when using social media or traditional media to speak with or speak out to a company:

✸ Begin the conversation in a courteous tone, and remember your words are going to be read or heard by another human who is just sitting at his or her desk doing his or her job, and the person initially reading your words or speaking to you on the phone is most likely not one of the decision makers in the company. Consider him or her a step on the ladder to work your way up. Ask to speak to the supervisor, and on up until you have the ear/ eyes of someone in public relations or a VP level. Keep notes on everything, and save all of your correspondence. And if you get the outcome you want, write a thank-you note and commend them publicly on Twitter or Facebook.

❖ On Facebook, make sure to tag the company's page from the status update on your wall, so that your friends and subscribers can follow the digital trail. And then copy and paste your statement directly into a comment on the company's wall. (Those comments may or may not be read by someone, so I also suggest following up with an e-mail to customer service or someone in public relations—most companies have a "contact us" page on their website.)

❖ On Twitter, make sure to use the correct Twitter handle for the company, and hashtag if there is one for the event (for example, during awareness-raising campaigns from Miss Representation the hashtag #NotBuyingIt is used). Tweets that contain a hashtag can then be called up in a batch, and you can watch the conversation unfold and meet like-minded activists.

❖ If you blog (or guest blog) about an action item or offensive product, take a minute to grab contact information from the company's website and include that in your post so your readers can move forward. Spread your post to your e-mail list and social media pages. Provide updates as the story progresses. Use keywords and have share buttons installed so that people can easily share your work. Also, provide links and pingbacks to other bloggers who have already covered the story and/or leave a supportive comment on their blog. You can also e-mail other bloggers with your post and offer for them to cross-post or share on their social media pages.

❖ If you use an online petition site, write a compelling letter and use a powerful graphic on the petition page. (There are sample letters you can read from winning campaigns on the site.) That graphic becomes the logo or branding of that initiative, and people will recognize it as they see it around the web. Blast Facebook and Twitter contacts with the petition link. Provide updates and keep the conversation going around the issue. I suggest using Change.org or Care 2's www.petitionsite.com.

❖ Use vlogging (video blogging) as a way to make your voice heard. This option is great for being able to show a product directly to your viewer, as opposed to trying to describe it with the written word. This is a great way to involve your kids, and interview other parents and their families. Your kids can give their opinions and contribute cue cards or illustrations they show to the camera. I find unscripted, organic vlogs to be the best. There are several online tutorials to help you set up a YouTube or Vimeo channel, or embed a video file into a blog site like Wordpress.

❋ Use traditional media such as a newspaper or television news to get the story out. Write a letter to the editor of a magazine or your local paper. Call or e-mail the newsroom at your local station and pitch the story. Most local TV news stations do human interest and consumer watchdog series, so ask them to cover this area you feel passionate about. Offer to invite your friends over so that they have a group to interview. Give them the name of the store manager you spoke with. Assemble a group of kids for the reporter to interview for their piece.

If you are approaching a chain store's staff directly, know that decisions about product selection and merchandising are typically made at the corporate level, so a store manager may not have the authority to move or remove an item or display from the floor. Retail products are bought by the purchasing department as much as six to twelve months in advance of the item hitting the sales floor, so make sure to get contact information for district managers and the purchasing department right away, before they begin buying for next season. My recommendations for talking to both decisions makers and those who report to them are:

1. Greet them with a smile and handshake, give them your name, and tell them why you would like their time. "Hi there, my name is Melissa Wardy. Could I take a minute of your time to discuss a concern I have about the girls' swimsuit selection this season? As a parent and frequent shopper, I'd really like for you to pass this along at your next team meeting or to your supervisor."

2. Make your "ask" known in the first minute of the conversation. Example: "Hi, Melanie, so nice to meet you. I'd like to borrow

your ear for a minute because I saw a sign in the girls' department that upset me and I'd like to talk to you quickly about why
and how we could get it moved." Or, "Hi, Jim. I know you are
the store manager and not in charge of buying, but I'd like to
follow up our conversation with an e-mail to you that I would
appreciate if you could forward to your buyers. It really means
a lot to my kids to be able to have choices in all colors, not just
pink or blue, for their bike helmets, and I just wanted to encourage your buyers to continue with this trend when they purchase
for next season."

3. If you and the person you are speaking with come to an
impasse, that is OK. Thank the employee for his or her time,
and ask for the customer relations phone number or the contact
information for the manager. I usually say something like, "I
really appreciate you hearing me out, and I realize we can't
resolve this here and now. But I'd like to convey my concerns
to your manager, and I'd also like to applaud your responsive-
ness while we talked. Would you please give me the contact
info for your manager?" If your request is refused, make note of
the employee's name from his or her nametag on your receipt,
along with the date, time, and store number. All this information will be helpful when you take your concern via phone
or e-mail up the chain to the company's consumer relations
department. If a store employee or manager was helpful or
considerate to you, make sure to mention their customer care
as you move forward.

4. As you move up the chain of command, keep a list of names and
titles. I have found it relatively easy to reach high-level people at
major corporations, and the key is to call with a concern (rather
than a complaint) and be friendly. You can deliver a strong argument without being rude, and as a consumer, you have every
right to provide feedback on your shopping experience. Even
if you really hate a product, act like a team player rather than
an adversary as you present your position. Most of the people
working at these places are also parents or have children in their

lives they care about. And more often than not, the individuals I talk to agree with our position.

5. When you get a positive result, write a thank-you note to the players involved. Thank them publicly on your social media sites when you update your friends on the story.

The following is a perfect example of how a company may receive and react to customer feedback. My friend Hillary Manaster, a team member at Sanford Harmony Program, was walking through Nordstrom one weekend when she saw a sign in the girls' department that bothered her, so she spoke up about it and got impressive results.

Dear Nordstrom,

I was recently shopping in the children's department at your Scottsdale, Arizona, location, and I was surprised and upset to see a sign hanging in the girls' section that read: BOYS STINK. I asked the sales clerk if anyone had complained about it yet. She told me, "no," and added that it was just meant to be cute. When I asked her if there was an equally negative sentiment about girls hanging in the boys' section, she told me, "no." She did share that she had overheard some young (male) shoppers complain to their parents that it wasn't fair that a GIRLS STINK sign wasn't hanging on the boys' side.

By no means am I writing to suggest that you make it "fair" by creating balanced slanderous signage. I am writing to point out that a sign that says BOYS STINK is really not cute at all. It's mean. And as a mother of two daughters, I'm just grateful that they are too young to read. As a retail store I realize you are not in the business of creating social change, but I do believe you are in the business of making customers feel good about themselves. Having a sign that tells half the population that they stink seems to me to be counterproductive.

I know some adults think that there is really no harm in pitting boys and girls against each other, but many of us see it in a different way. Many of us hope to see our kids (boys and girls) developing kind, caring relationships with one another. Many of us would like for our kids to grow up without negative feelings about the other gender.

Many of us would like for our kids to not be exposed to such antiquated gender attitudes, stereotypes, and biases. But above all, I think most of us would like for our kids to be nice. Telling boys that they stink is not nice—any child over the age of two could tell you that.

I realize that some people may feel that I am overreacting, but I don't think I'm off base expecting your company to treat all of your customers with respect. After all, Nordstrom is known for outstanding customer service. I'm quite certain your company would never authorize a sign reading WOMEN SUCK to hang in the men's department. So it seems logical for Nordstrom to use the same consideration for their youngest customers as well. Don't you agree?

Sincerely,
Hillary L. Manaster, M.Ed.
Sanford Harmony Program
School of Social and Family Dynamics
Arizona State University

Nordstrom is well known for exemplary customer service, listening to customer feedback, and acting on it. The same day Hillary received this e-mail in reply:

Hello Hillary,

Thank you for taking the time to share your feedback. Our customers' opinions are very important to Nordstrom and greatly assist us with our continued efforts to provide the best merchandise and service to our customers.

I think you have made a very good point in showing how to set a good example for all our customers. Please know that I will share your experience and feedback, so that we learn and improve. If you need anything else, please do not hesitate to contact me.

Regards,
[Name Redacted]
Customer Service Specialist
Nordstrom

Now, that sounds a little like corporate-ese, and there was no follow-up plan in place, so it's possible to interpret that letter as being blown off. However, three days later, Hillary received another e-mail from a director-level staff member at Nordstrom:

Dear Ms. Manaster,

On behalf of Nordstrom . . . I'd like to apologize. We're so sorry this sign offended you.

We have one rule, and that's to use good judgment. We didn't do so when we posted those signs. We were attempting to be whimsical and kid-friendly, but we realize now that what we posted wasn't that. For that we apologize.

The signs have been removed from your store and we're working to have them removed from other stores as well.

We apologize that our original response to you from our customer service specialist missed the mark. We've addressed that as well.

Sincerely,
[Name Redacted]
Nordstrom

Now *that* is some customer service! It is fair to say not all such interactions will have this positive of an outcome. But what if Hillary had never spoken up? There would still be a large pink sign hanging in the girls' department that reads BOYS STINK. Your voice, even if it is only one voice, can have a strong impact.

I know it is easier to shrug and walk away, or have the mind-set that this doesn't affect your kid so it isn't your problem. But it is our problem. There is an injustice being done to childhood and the tiny people who inhabit it. Who better to speak up than us? We are all capable of taking up this fight—including our kids.

Activist Kids

Get your kids involved in speaking out against products or marketing messages they don't agree with. Amelia wrote her first concerned consumer letter to the dolphins at Sea World (we mailed it to Sea World, attention: Dolphins) when she was four and a half years old. A week later we received the most amazing thank-you letter from the trainers and a large packet of educational materials from Sea World's marketing department. She now regularly writes letters whenever she feels the need to get something off her chest. In doing so she has learned that she has a voice and that she will be listened to.

Kids can make videos, start a blog, use social media (if over the age of thirteen and with supervision), write e-mails, draw or write letters, ask you to transcribe a letter, offer product suggestions or improvements, and more. If marketers are trying to turn our kids into mini-consumers, let's play their game and turn our kids into conscientious consumers.

Letters from the Experts
Dana Edell

Dana Edell is the executive director of SPARK Movement, an intergenerational, girl-fueled activist movement fighting to end the sexualization of girls. Formerly the cofounder and director of viBe Theater Experience, Dana has directed more than sixty plays and produced seven CDs of music all written and performed by teenage girls in New York City about the issues they face daily.

Letter from a childless ally:

Sometimes when folks ask me if I have children, I say that I have hundreds of teenage daughters. Now before you moms and dads scoff and clench and simmer that I cannot claim parentage without surviving feedings and cryings and bullyings, let me make my case. I have seen and heard teenage girls in ways that parents sometimes never do. For the past fifteen years, girls have been telling me the stories of their lives—their fears, insecurities, sex lives, friend dramas, parent pressures, heartbreaks, loves, and desires. I was thrilled when Melissa invited me to write about why I am so committed to guiding and inspiring girls to scrub their metaphorical glasses and see through the sexy-tinted sludge that our culture and media has been bombarding them with.

I am committed to ending the sexualization of girls because I have seen the absurd and horrifying ways that teenage girls get sucked into making choices to be "sexy" in very narrow definitions of "sexy" (guess the body type, heel height, and skirt length I'm referring to!). I watch girls choose manicures over soccer practice, calorie counting over dancing, and boyfriends over best friends. And yet in spite of the avalanche of images of "perfect," "sexed-up" girls that bat eyelashes from billboards, Barbie boxes, and music videos, I am here to tell you about girls like Carina and Alice and YingYing and Eliana and Sariel and Julia who grew up in this world where three-year-olds are plucked and rouged and squeezed into minidresses.

And yet these young women found the tools to fight back. They saw the potential dangers of a world where little girls are given makeup kits and curling irons while their brothers lay the bricks for city hall. And instead of rolling their eyes or groaning internally, these girls took action. Since you bought this book and you've read this far, I already know that you are a hip, enlightened parent who is probably not registering your daughter for Little Miss Beauty Pageant (unless of course you've already been scheming about how to subvert the contest, win the prize money, and deposit it into her college bank account). As an ally for girl activists, my advice to the parents out there is to provide the spaces and resources for your daughters to not just recognize the injustices in the world around them but to do something about it. With guidance from passionate and loving adults, Julia wrote a petition that changed the teen magazine industry, Alice made a series of videos, Eliana plastered Post-it notes to offensive Halloween costumes, YingYing wrote a blog that inserted her voice into the conversation about "slut-shaming," Carina gave a speech to four hundred girls encouraging them to love their unique colors and bodies despite the racist, sizeist, and sexist messages they get from the media.

My wish for our future is that you encourage your kids to change the world so that when my daughter is born, we're a little bit closer to living in a world where girls and boys can grow into the strong, compassionate, brilliant, unique, and loving people we know they can be! I fully support the amazing work Melissa has done with redefining girly and cannot wait for the world in which this book is required reading for anyone thinking about raising a child.

With SPARKs,
Dana

Becoming the Media You Want to See

Families are under no obligation to accept the media presented to them. I encourage my own children to think critically about commercials, advertisements, catalogs, cartoons, toys, books, music, and movies. That doesn't mean we do not enjoy media. It just means we think about and challenge the media our family takes in, and if we don't like it, we create our own.

Getting kids to think critically about media comes a lot more naturally than you may think. I get dozens of e-mails every day from parents asking, "How do I teach . . . ?" or "What do I say . . . ?" My answer is always this: Ask commonsense questions, and then listen to your kids' responses. A few examples:

"Those girls are making fun of her outfit. Are they acting like a kind friend?"

"That movie preview only had one girl in the story. Does that seem weird to you there is only one girl?"

"All of the superheroes in this show are boys. Do you think the writers could have made some of them girls?"

"This magazine ad says I need this product to be beautiful. Do you think a cream can make a person beautiful?"

There is no secret or trick to doing it. We just question stuff all of the time. Now I overhear the kids doing it with each other when they watch television together. We don't watch a lot of TV, but they do have a couple of favorite shows with positive story lines that show male and female characters working together. I know my messages are sinking in when they turn off the TV halfway through the show to role-play the story themselves, creating their own media. Amelia and Benny have no trouble assimilating any character to fit their story. Amelia will often take the role of a male character she was watching, or she will make a hybrid character of her own to be a female hero. Benny will take on the role of a female character without batting an eye; in his mind women are heroes.

I am often asked, "What is the right age of the child to start this kind of dialogue?" Around age two (according to the American Academy of Pediatrics, kids shouldn't be watching TV younger than this anyway), kids can follow along as together you ask and answer your own questions. For example, when Amelia was two and three she loved the Wonder Pets. As we watched together, I would say things like, "Amelia, I think Ming Ming was very brave to save her friends. Wasn't Ming Ming being a good friend?" At two years old Amelia was still learning the concept of friendship, but now she was also learning to think about and unpack the media she was watching. Instead of just sitting there and taking it in like a sponge, she was acting more like a colander, sifting the messages before letting them through.

How Kids Can Make Their Own Media

Here are some ways that kids can create or shape their own media:

Birth–age 2

❉ Baby sign language is an excellent way to let your little one express herself before she has the verbal skills to do so. It allows her to interpret and share her view of the world. It allows the parent to ask more complex questions that build on what the child is observing, which is a key component to media literacy. Your local library or pediatrician will be able to give you resources for your family to learn baby sign language.

  Example: You and baby are out on a stroller ride, and you see a dog. Most parents would say, "Do you see the dog, sweetie?" But when your baby is able to initiate conversation and sign to you that she sees a dog, you get to go a step further and say, "I see the doggie too. I like the brown and white spots by his eye. Where is your eye?"

❉ Start framing a positive body image for her in her very earliest years, when she is just discovering her body. Talk about her smart mind, strong arms and legs, healthy tummy, and warm smile, and talk about what she can do with all those amazing parts of her body.

❉ Engaging in messy, tactile art projects starting at about eighteen months old is a great way for your girl to learn she can create something that has lasting power while at the same time building concentration and motor skills. Finger paint, shaving cream, and chunky crayons are good for the little ones. We hang all of our kids' artwork at their eye level, which encourages them to go back, review the art, and build on the story it tells.

❉ Through songs and clapping rhythms, a baby can learn to repeat and to change what she hears. Even singing a song but being silly about the lyrics will get her to think critically about what she is hearing, and compare that to knowledge she has about how something is supposed to be.

Example: Amelia used to love this from fifteen months on: we would sit and sing while she was in the tub, but I would mess up the words to "Old McDonald" by singing, "Old McDonald had a circus, ee-i-ee-i-o." Amelia would go nuts and shake her head, and I would try over and over again to get it right. When I did, she would clap for her ridiculous mother, and then listen very intently for the next time I messed up. So in the next verse I would add a gorilla to the farm, which would send Amelia into hysterics because gorillas don't live on farms. "No, Mommy! Do right!" she would say, and then clap for me when I got my act together.

Ages 2–4

- ❁ At this age kids can answer simple questions about a TV show or movie they are watching. Ask about the characters' feelings, how one of their actions would make another feel, the characters' behavior, the number of female characters, whether a different character could be doing the hero's job, and so on.

- ❁ Paint, finger paint, or draw/color a picture about a story she wants to tell or idea she has. Transcribe the story for her, write her name and the date, and attach it to the bottom of the paper. Display it somewhere in your home as this shows the child her ideas and words hold meaning to the people around her.

- ❁ Make up silly songs or mix up lyrics to songs your kids are familiar with (can also be done with stories) as sort of an ad lib, impromptu comedy. This teaches them that media can be fluid and that they can have influence over stories.

- ❁ Hold puppet shows or plays with stuffed animals to retell a story (particularly useful with princess stories that need reframing) or role-play a situation as a teachable moment.

- ❁ Read together each day, and allow your daughter to change the story's plot. I have friends who change fairy tales as they read to be more empowering, and my daughter likes to make up her own plot additions when reading chapter books that really get her imagination going.

Ages 5–9

- ❋ Help them to create simple story boards or books with art supplies from home. My kids love to create comic strips on the whiteboard that is set at their height in our dining room. Another favorite is cutting some plain white computer paper in half, stapling it together into a booklet, and letting them create their own books.
- ❋ We read a lot of books in our house, especially at bedtime, but one of the things my kids go nuts for are "Tuck stories," named after our always-in-trouble puppy, Tuck. My husband tells the story, and the kids interject what should happen next or introduce new characters or create new adventures or trouble our puppy finds himself in. My husband doesn't always remember where they left off, but the kids have the story locked in their minds. Being a storyteller is an important gift, and by working as a team my husband and the kids are creating their own media.
- ❋ This is a really crucial age to keep asking those critical thinking questions about characters and their actions in media—why the hero had to be a boy instead of a girl and so on. Then ask your daughter how she would change things up if she were the writer or producer.
- ❋ Find an old digital camera or camcorder for your kids to learn what it is like to be the creative director behind the lens. Amelia has proven herself to be a very good photojournalist, even if her beat is just our backyard. Benny loves to make movies. Letting the kids have a device that allows them to produce and watch their own media allows them to tell rich and layered stories. They can cast their playmates or the family dog in a role, create a set and costumes, and write and rewrite the "script." Equally important is that they can share this media and watch how it impacts others.
- ❋ Kids this age can start to speak out against (or for) media they feel strongly about. Maybe they really love a musician and her

song lyrics, or are really concerned that animals used in a film might have been injured during production. Show them how to find contact information and speak out.

Ages 10 and up

❀ Engage in activism. If your daughter is upset about a product or piece of media, encourage her to create what it is she feels was missing or voice what she would like to see. Encourage her to see something as not only impacting her but impacting all kids. Ask her questions like how she would like to see something done differently, what would she change if she were a player on this project, or what would she like to say to the audience viewing the piece of media she is concerned about.

❀ Encourage her to research, fact-check, and locate contact information to speak out.

❀ Encourage her to use blogging, vlogging, or adult-supervised social media to spread her message.

❀ Kids this age can be pretty passionate about issues, so help them put on their own fashion show that focuses on healthy body image, write a television newscast on issues they think should be covered, make a short film about human rights or an endangered animal, compose a letter to the editor, and so on.

❀ Get your girl involved in community theater, but not just acting onstage. The backstage/production side of it can be a valuable learning experience that gets her working with her hands and trying on management roles.

❀ Provide the resources and encouragement she needs to write her own music or plays, such as a cool notebook wrapped lovingly and decorated with some freshly sharpened pencils tied up in the ribbon with a note that reads, "I believe you have some of the best ideas around."

❀ Keep the critical thinking questions going when taking in media. Your daughter's peer group is very influential at this age, so include questions about her friendships.

Example: You and your tween are watching a show where there is some "mean girl" behavior. You have talked about this with her before, but this time ask questions like, "You know, those girls seem to enjoy being cruel to one another. Do your friends ever act that way, or do you accept one another's differences?"

❋ Keep a pack of sticky notes and a marker in your purse and your daughter's backpack so that you both can leave encouraging messages on mirrors, like, "See how beautiful you are?" or "You are beautiful every day, the media can never take that away." For more inspiring messages, check out the book *Operation Beautiful: Transforming the Way You See Yourself One Post-it Note at a Time* by Caitlin Boyle.

Letters from the Experts

Margot Magowan

Margot Magowan is the mother of three girls and blogs about media and feminism at ReelGirl.com.

❋ ❋ ❋

Dear Parents,

As the parents of three daughters, we are writing a middle-grades adventure-fantasy book featuring many strong, female characters. Dan, a landscaper, started telling this story to our daughters and they couldn't get enough of it. I'm a writer and started to help him write it all down. Now, it's become something we do together, and we are proud to have our daughters see us creating powerful and creative media for girls. Dan says, "Movies and books are a place where characters do extraordinary things. Women and girls should be allowed to do extraordinary acts and dream big."

> Lucy, age nine, says, "Girls are always the people who fall in love. Girls need some action."
>
> Alice, age six, says, "Boys are always the main character, and I want a girl to be the main character. My favorite color is black, not pink."
>
> Rose, age three, says, "My favorite color is golden, and I am Batgirl, not Batman."
>
> Love,
> The Magowan-Garvin Family

In addition to changing and creating her own media, your daughter can also repackage the messages coming at her. Here are some projects that you can do with your daughter one-on-one, as a family, or during a time when she has friends over. (Note: These are geared to ages six and up, but younger kids can still help you with projects like these. At the end of each project are instructions for ages five and under.)

"I Am . . ." Silhouette

Have your daughter lie down on the sidewalk or a large piece of butcher paper and trace her body's outline with chalk or crayons. Fill her silhouette by having her write or help her to write words that reflect who she is: her character, her likes and interests, her talents and strengths. Doodle around the words, or if using paper add color by adding glitter, yarn hair, or even photographs of her being full of awesome. This would make a great decoration for the back of her bedroom door.

Itty-Bitty Version: She will have fun being traced; give her chalk or crayons to "help" you. Explain to her step by step what you are doing and what the words that you are writing mean. Keep her engaged by asking her to point to all of her strong and healthy body parts. This is something you can hang in her room and talk to her about each night when you put her to bed.

Time Capsule Message

This can be done either by writing letters or by video blog, and you can do this a number of ways—you and your daughter can write letters to read to each other or to yourselves in ten to fifteen years, write letters to the childhood version of you to be read on your birthday ten years from now, write a letter to your daughter's future children, or write a letter that you think your ninety-nine-year-old self would want you to know when you are twenty. Have your letters focus on what you want you to know or remember through the various phases of life. The point is to focus on having our goals, wishes, and dreams far outlast anything the media has to say as we see our entire life as a project that we continue improving on.

Itty-Bitty Version: Small children do not understand the concept of time, but they do understand making wishes on birthday candles each year. Ask them to help you think of birthday wishes for different parts of her life. Maybe instead of writing a letter with a little one, decorate a paper birthday cake and write a wish on each candle that we should remember no matter what age we are.

"You Are Special Because . . ." Mobile

Cut out shapes like clouds, hearts, airplanes, stars, or baseballs from card stock and write an attribute that you see in your daughter on each one. Have a couple of blank shapes for her to add her own words. Explain why you chose each word and how she embodies it. Set out a buffet of art supplies (glitter, sequins, feathers, ribbon, fancy paper, paint, oil pastels) and ask her to help you decorate each shape and cut the ribbon to hang them. Hang these from a ribbon or string from a central hoop or series of twigs. Suspend the mobile above her bed or desk so that she has a visual reminder of all of the amazing qualities you see in her.

Itty-Bitty Version: Make a couple of extra blank shapes that she can go to town decorating. When it comes time to hang the mobile from the ceiling, pick her up and let her do the honors.

"My Dreams" Vision Board

Find foam board or a blank canvas at an art supply store. Start by working out on paper what dreams and goals your daughter would like to put on here, and how she would like to organize them (in a big collage, right now dreams / forever dreams, or this school year / this summer / a year from now, etc.). Gather all the materials she will need to assemble it, put on some good music, and have some healthy snacks nearby. Make a board of your own! Find a special spot in her room where she will be able to see her vision board on a daily basis, and check back in with her from time to time on how she is approaching and achieving her goals.

Itty-Bitty Version: Make a list of special things she wants on her wish board, and either draw or cut from magazines pictures that represent her goals. Maybe a giraffe for "grow tall," or a photograph of her sneakers for "put on my shoes by myself." Or put paint on her hands to make handprints, let dry, and then attach a piece of paper with her goal written down. When she reaches her goal, take a photograph of her and add it to the hand.

Theme Song Party

Invite over some special friends and their moms, or cousins and aunties, for a girl power dance party night. Plan a craft or a nighttime hike by flashlight or a pedicure station or a science experiment. Spend the evening dancing and listening to girl power anthems (*A Mighty Girl* has a huge list: www.amightygirl.com) and spending quality time together. Let the girls decide where conversation goes, and have some healthy snacks on hand.

Itty-Bitty Version: Shorten the time on this, as young children's attention spans will be shorter. Pick three or four songs to jam to, and then finish with a bubble bath or a quick art project like a self-portrait.

"Our Founding Mothers" Reading and Art Project

Chances are your daughter will spend a lot of time in school studying the men who shaped our country (or any country) and very little about the women who did. Supplement that with trips to the library or Internet searches to learn about our founding mothers. Read together, and discuss what challenges, hardships, or benefits of sisterhood these women would have faced in their times. Try to re-create period dress from the past, or have your daughter pretend to be a historical figure and write a short speech. Fill a sketchpad with doodles and questions and ideas that come up. Use cardboard boxes to re-create Amelia Earhart's airplane or Marie Curie's laboratory.

Itty-Bitty Version: Get books geared toward young children about women in history, such as *My Name Is Not Isabella* by Jennifer Fosberry or *Amelia to Zora: Twenty-Six Women Who Changed the World* by Cynthia Chin-Lee.

"Beauty Comes from the Family Tree" Collage

Make copies of family photos going back as many generations as you can find. Create a tree out of card stock or foam board, then assemble a tree of beauty that has been passed down between the generations. Label each picture with the woman's name and something special about her. Talk about where her dark hair or long fingers come from, and how her genes and her confidence are what make her beautiful. For girls who are adopted, switch out genetic traits for actions that made these women beautiful, and by your daughter's photo put plans she has to be beautiful through actions just like the women in her forever family.

Itty-Bitty Version: Show pictures of grandma, you, and baby as young children, teenagers, and now to show her how people change as they grow, but the beauty always remains.

"Empowering Word" Typography Collage

Find some scrapbooking papers with beautiful patterns, then ink or paint empowering words on them to create a collage. Decoupage them onto an old table, a framed mirror, or a vase.

Itty-Bitty Version: Buy a couple sets of alphabet magnets. Write a list of empowering words and place them in a sheet protector. While you make dinner or work from home, have your little one copy the list with her magnets on the fridge, or just line up the letters over the words from your list.

"I Am Full of Awesome" Digital Photo Book

Take photos of your girl doing full-of-awesome active, brave, artistic, funny things and create a digital photo book. Write captions that describe her feelings while she was doing whatever is shown in the photo and why she is proud of herself. Surprise her with a couple of photos with captions from her siblings or grandparents or best friend.

Itty-Bitty Version: There is a good chance that adults or other family members will be in her photos, so add their names in capital letters in the captions so that she learns name recognition and family faces.

"A Year of Empowerment" Calendar and Mixed Media

Decide on twelve empowering words, one for each month of the year. Create visual images to represent each word or use mixed media to decorate twelve eight-and-a-half-by-eleven-inch sheets of paper. Print out a calendar template and take all of the pages to be bound at an office store. Take time on a quiet night or on the weekends to write down awesome things or messages of daily gratitude in the margins of the calendar.

Itty-Bitty Version: Instead of a calendar, make laminated placemats that she can choose from at mealtime. Keep them on a low shelf or drawer so that she can get them out herself and place them on the table.

How Parents Can Make Their Own Media

As parents, we can also create our own media. I launched my blog and business after I saw a gap in empowering messages for little girls. In under three years' time, I have shipped my products to all fifty states and over fifteen countries. My blog holds hundreds of posts with nearly a million views, and at the time of this writing I have more than nineteen thousand social media followers. And you are just about to finish reading my book. I am a mom with two small kids who works out of her dining room. Anything is possible.

If you have an idea for a blog or a product, go after it. I really enjoy being my own boss, and the feedback I receive from my customers keeps my fire lit to strive to do better for our kids every day. I am frequently asked for new products that I just don't have the capacity to produce at this time, but the demand is there, and I intend for Pigtail Pals & Ballcap Buddies to grow and fill it. Some of the most successful children's products were created by parents who saw a gap in the market and created something to fill that hole. I get asked for swimsuits, Halloween costumes, bedroom decor, underwear, toys, and birthday cards. Clearly my company has a lot of room to grow. That means other small businesses do too.

My business started in a notebook, but with the economy heading south I knew I wanted to stay online and operate an e-commerce site as opposed to a brick-and-mortar store. I researched what store platforms were most user-friendly, as well as payment processors and shipping vendors. I vetted my apparel vendors and print shop. I studied the Consumer Products Safety Improvement Act (CPSIA) regulations and found artists for my work. I networked and sent out press releases and took to learning social media like it was a second language. I wrote a business plan, got my state licenses and a tax ID number, and secured a loan from my bank. None of it was easy. All of it was worth it.

There are so many ways for parents to start creating and changing the way media and products look for our children. There is risk involved in starting out on a new venture, and I went over two years before I gave myself my first paycheck. Many nights I worked until 2:00 AM and was up at 6:00 AM to start a new day with the kids. I was desperate for sleep and determined to make this idea work. I believed in it, and I believed in myself. I was told by a children's-line rep at a buyers' market that my apparel was ahead of the curve and wouldn't sell—three weeks before selling $18,000 worth of T-shirts in a month.

Letters from the Experts

Michele Yulo

Michele Yulo is the creator and owner of Princess Free Zone, Inc., and the author of *Super Tool Lula: The Bully-Fighting Super Hero*. She writes a blog about gender issues including identity and stereotypes specifically related to children with a focus on preventing bullying.

Dear Parents,

"Redefining girly" for me has been both a very personal mission and a professional vision. As the mother of a little girl who has wanted nothing to do with all things princess since the age of three, I became motivated to be part of a movement that works to eliminate gender stereotypes that say all girls are the same.

Initially frustrated by the lack of choice I was finding for my daughter—who adamantly refused to wear pink, play with dolls, or don a dress—I shopped in boy departments for the primary-colored clothing she liked and for the dinosaur designs she preferred. She got funny looks from people as we picked out her outfits in boy departments. And when she decided to cut her hair short, she put up with the often snide comments and questions about her choices.

So I created Princess Free Zone, Inc., which, like Pigtail Pals & Ballcap Buddies, hopes to show the world that being a girl is not confined to one version of femininity but recognizes that there are infinite ways to be a girl. We need to make the world a place where children can feel comfortable exploring their identities and being themselves, but to do this there needs to be change about how people view gender.

This is a huge task as it seeks to tackle many fronts including long-held institutionalized beliefs about gender by individuals that inevitably spill over into the often-intrusive presence of corporate marketing and advertising that continues to separate boy play and girl play into blue and pink environments. Children absorb these messages subliminally and by the time they start school have very rigid ideas about what it means to be a boy or a girl.

I truly believe we can do this. I believe it is necessary to the health and well-being of every child. Melissa Wardy believes it too, and I appreciate her hard work and determination to allow all children the ability to experience childhoods free from a culture that pushes them to grow up too fast and too soon.

Sincerely and with thanks,
Michele Yulo

Letters from the Experts

Jodi Norgaard

Jodi Norgaard has always been involved in sports and for many years was a coach for Girls on the Run. She now owns and operates Go! Go! Sports Girls, a line of soft dolls with an athletic theme.

Dear Parents,

Two experiences led to my inspiration to create the Go! Go! Sports Girl Dolls. For four years I coached Girls on the Run, in which my daughter participated. It is an amazing program that teaches girls confidence through running. I saw the program change the lives of not only the young girls, but mine too.

The second experience wasn't as uplifting. When my daughter was nine years old I wanted to purchase a doll for her. Many of the dolls I saw on the market sent an inappropriate message: grow up fast, wear short skirts, and put on makeup. This frustrated me and made me angry. So I decided to do something about it by creating my own doll that would encourage young girls to embrace and enjoy their true age. My hope is that the Go! Go! Sports Girls help deliver the right message.

My daughter, Grace, who is now sixteen, has joined me in a few interviews, and one question she answered is very memorable. Last year she was asked: "What is your opinion on the way tween-teen girls are portrayed in the media?" Grace's response: "The media portrays us a lot differently than we really are. We are not crazy, wild, and hard to control. They portray us as sexy and we are just girls, just people. The media likes to tell us who we are. They don't define us! It's unfair." I like her answer!

Always remember that change is never made by mainstream ideas.

Dream Big and Go For It!
Jodi

I network and collaborate frequently with like-minded businesses and colleagues. I support and promote Kickstarter campaigns for new, healthy products and media for kids. Kickstarter and Indiegogo are two great crowdsourcing sites to get a project off the ground. Etsy is a great site for selling handmade goods. Society 6 is a collaborative artist site that allows you to post artwork and photography in a shop page that they then turn into products for you for a small commission.

Once you get into this space, you quickly find out small business own-ers are passionate about what we do and welcome new businesses and products that share a passion for honoring childhood.

Parents have been responsible for changing products in the mar-ketplace and lobbying for changes in legislation that affects our chil-dren. My hope is that after reading this book you will make changes in your family. Maybe you need to shift the way you approach body image; maybe you need to be more vigilant with media consumption. Hopefully now you have a working script for how to explain sexualized products to your children, or you feel better supported in not giving in to the trend in sexualized clothing or toys.

Whatever takeaways you gain from the book, know that they are changes or ideas worth the investment of your time. You are your daughter's greatest champion. When she came into your life, you looked into her tiny face and promised to love and protect her. Part of being a child today means being protected from the commercializa-tion, sexualization, and gendered messages that have invaded child-hood. Be your daughter's hero. Be the person who stands up for her and demands she has a right to her girlhood. Raise her to know that she is smart, daring, and adventurous. Raise her to reject the messages the media is trying to trick her into believing about herself. Raise her to know that she has a voice and the right to take up space in this world.

Raise her in such a way that twenty years from now the girls of her generation will have reshaped our world in such a significant manner that they will pick up this book and look at one another in bewilder-ment and say, "Can you believe it ever used to be this way?"

Acknowledgments

Writing this book has been a time of reflection for me on how I spent the days of my girlhood and the loving family and mentors I had around me. I have been blessed to be surrounded by women who are intelligent, articulate, daring, and accomplished. Because of their influence throughout my life it has never occurred to me to live any other way.

I have to start by thanking Jess Weiner for literally kicking me under the table and telling me that I had a book waiting in my heart. She believed in me at a time when I was trying to figure out where I fit in this space of girl empowerment and parent coaching, and that has meant everything.

That encouragement led to my saying yes when my wonderful editor, Lisa Reardon, contacted me about working with Chicago Review Press. I had no idea how to write a book or that the process was so similar to giving birth, but Lisa has been an amazing midwife throughout.

I have had the privilege of being mentored by people whom I have looked up to for years, and it seems surreal to be able to call them my mentors, colleagues, and, most important, my friends. Lyn Mikel Brown and Peggy Orenstein, I am a better woman and mother because of you, and I thank you for the guidance and support you have shown me.

It is very special to love what you do and to get to work in the same field, often side by side, with some of the best people working to end sexualization and stereotyping. Nancy Gruver, Jennifer Hartstein, Amy Jussel, Susan Linn, Elena Rossini, Jennifer Shewmaker, Jennifer Siebel Newsom, Robyn Silverman, Rachel Simmons, Collett Smart, Melinda Tankard Reist, Marci Warhaft-Nadler, Ines Almeida, and Rosalind Wiseman are some of the most talented and dedicated people I have had the honor to work with, and I hold so much respect for you all.

Thank you to Veronica Arreola, Dana Edell, Melanie Klein, Avital Norman Nathman, Jennifer Pozner, and Megan Williams for showing me the path to what feminist activism and feminist motherhood look like.

Much gratitude to Lori Day, Carrie Goldman, Rebecca Hains, Margot Magowan, Hillary Manaster, Jodi Norgaard, Crystal Smith, and Michelle Yulo for being my sounding boards and sanity savers, and mothers who are daring to make a difference for our kids. It is such an honor to work with you and see our efforts shifting the way people parent.

Special thanks for the valuable work and research from the Sanford Harmony Program and the Geena Davis Institute on Gender in Media.

This book would not have been written without the amazing experience and experiment that is the Pigtail Pals & Ballcap Buddies Facebook community, some nineteen thousand people strong. Every day we show up to push boundaries and have conversations like no one else is having and we do so coming from different perspectives and experiences and always maintain a level of respect and teaching. I am continuously impressed with what we are doing there, and I have the messages and letters from hundreds of parents to prove that by aggregating our voices, we are making a difference. Thank you for being not silent with me.

Special shout-outs to Tanya Burns, Kate Griffiths, Brandy King, Emily Marymont-Sexton, Meghan Mascoro-Jackson, Erica Mason,

Laurie Miles, Shelby Packer, Gabrielle Tenn New, Robyn Widmer, and Jennifer Williams.

You can't get through life without good girlfriends: Cheri Diehls, Tina Jorgenson, Lexi Monroe, Sara Schumacher, and Courtney Siel-off, I owe all of you a very large party. Lori B., Michelle C., Kris H., Stacy H., Jennie K., Sheri L., Rachel McC., Erin S., and Kelly S., thank you for always supporting me. To Jennifer Jacura and Bil Simser—I love you guys.

This book was written because my amazing babysitter Camry gave up her summer to come tend to my darlings while I escaped to the Hedberg Public Library and Mocha Moments. We love you, Camry!

Enormous chunks of this book were written while I was sitting on my parents' living room couch, a total of ten weekends spent in peace and quiet so that I could focus. Mom and Dad, there really aren't words to say thank you for everything. All that I am is a reflection of what amazing parents you are. I so deeply appreciate your unwavering support and love.

The love of my family means everything—Aunt Nancy, Eric, Lisa, Christopher, Shannon, Aunt Phyllis, Sally, Jennifer, and Amanda, thank you. Grandma Jean and Grandma Sally—your voices are in my heart every day.

To Jason—Mr. Pigtail Pals—you have shown me support, love, and patience during this project. Most important, you believe in me and the importance of this message for all these little girls. Thank you for taking on so much extra work around the house and with the kids while I worked on these chapters. SHMILY.

And finally, to Amelia and Benny—you are my cubs. I love you much too much. You have been so patient and so good while I worked on this project. All of this was for the two of you. I am so proud of you both. And guess what? With this sentence, the book is done! *Let's go play!*

Resources

What to Read

Bullied: What Every Parent, Teacher, and Kid Needs to Know About Ending the Cycle of Fear by Carrie Goldman

The Case for Make Believe: Saving Play in a Commercialized World by Susan Linn

Cinderella Ate My Daughter: Dispatches from the Front Lines of the New Girlie-Girl Culture by Peggy Orenstein

The Curse of the Good Girl: Raising Authentic Girls with Courage and Confidence by Rachel Simmons

The Gender Trap: Parents and the Pitfalls of Raising Boys and Girls by Emily W. Kane

Good Girls Don't Get Fat: How Weight Obsession Is Screwing Up Our Girls and What We Can Do to Help Them Thrive Despite It by Robyn J. A. Silverman and Dina Santorelli

Packaging Girlhood: Rescuing Our Daughters from Marketers' Schemes by Sharon Lamb and Lyn Mikel Brown

Pink Brain, Blue Brain: How Small Differences Grow into Troublesome Gaps—and What We Can Do About It by Lise Eliot

Pornland: How Porn Has Hijacked Our Sexuality by Gail Dines

Princess Recovery: A How-To Guide to Raising Strong, Empowered Girls Who Can Create Their Own Happily Ever Afters by Jennifer Hartstein

The Purity Myth: How America's Obsession with Virginity Is Hurting Young Women by Jessica Valenti

Queen Bees and Wannabes: Helping Your Daughter Survive Cliques, Gossip, Boyfriends, and the New Realities of Girl World by Rosalind Wiseman

Reality Bites Back: The Troubling Truth About Guilty Pleasure TV by Jennifer L. Pozner

Reviving Ophelia: Saving the Selves of Adolescent Girls by Mary Pipher

So Sexy So Soon: The New Sexualized Childhood and What Parents Can Do to Protect Their Kids by Diane E. Levin and Jean Kilbourne

A Very Hungry Girl: How I Filled Up on Life . . . and How You Can Too! by Jessica Weiner

Who to Turn To

Melissa Atkins Wardy

www.pigtailpals.com

Owner of Pigtail Pals & Ballcap Buddies online boutique, parent activist, educator, and blogger (http://blog.pigtailpals.com). And author of the book you're holding!

Michele Borba

http://micheleborba.com

Education psychologist and expert on children, teens, parenting, bullying, and moral development; author of twenty-two books including *The Big Book of Parenting Solutions: 101 Answers to Your Everyday Challenges and Wildest Worries.*

Lyn Mikel Brown

www.packaginggirlhood.com

Professor at Colby College, member APA Psychology of Women Executive Board, activist and mentor, and author (with Sharon Lamb) of

Packaging Girlhood: Rescuing Our Daughters from Marketers' Schemes and *Meeting at the Crossroads: Women's Psychology and Girls' Development.*

Carrie Goldman
www.carriegoldmanauthor.com
Parent-activist, author of *Bullied: What Every Parent, Teacher, and Kid Needs to Know About Ending the Cycle of Fear.* Blogs at www.chicago now.com/portrait-of-an-adoption.

Rebecca Hains
www.rebeccahains.com
Media studies professor and author of *Growing Up with Girl Power: Girlhood on Screen and in Everyday Life.* Blogs about children's media culture at www.rebeccahains.wordpress.com.

Jennifer Hartstein
www.drjen.com
Child and adolescent psychologist, author of *Princess Recovery: A How-To Guide to Raising Strong, Empowered Girls Who Can Create Their Own Happily Ever Afters.*

Amy Jussel
www.shapingyouth.org
Founder and director of Shaping Youth, a nonprofit consortium using the power of media for positive change.

Jean Kilbourne
www.jeankilbourne.com
Education psychologist, director of the *Killing Us Softly* documentary series, author (with Diane E. Levin) of *So Sexy So Soon: The New Sexualized Childhood and What Parents Can Do to Protect Their Kids.*

Susan Linn
www.consumingkids.com
Cofounder and director of the coalition Campaign for a Commercial-Free Childhood, instructor in psychiatry at Harvard Medical School,

and author of *The Case for Make Believe: Saving Play in a Commercialized World*.

Peggy Orenstein
http://peggyorenstein.com
A contributing writer for the *New York Times Magazine* and the author of *Cinderella Ate My Daughter: Dispatches from the Front Lines of the New Girlie-Girl Culture*; *Waiting for Daisy: A Tale of Two Continents, Three Religions, Five Fertility Doctors, an Oscar, an Atomic Bomb, a Romantic Night, and One Woman's Quest to Become a Mother*; *Flux: Women on Sex, Work, Kids, Love, and Life in a Half-Changed World*; and the classic *Schoolgirls: Young Women, Self-Esteem, and the Confidence Gap*.

Debbie Reber
www.debbiereber.com
Speaker and Gen-Y life coach who helps girls and women connect with their true purpose: to live more authentic, inspired, and fulfilling lives; author of *In Their Shoes: Extraordinary Women Describe Their Amazing Careers*; *Love, Love, Love: Language of Love and Cupidity* (stories for young adults); and the teen self-help series *Chicken Soup for the Teenage Soul: The Real Deal*.

Jennifer Shewmaker
www.jennifershewmaker.com
Author of a forthcoming book on children, sex, and the media (forthcoming fall 2014) and owner of the *Operation Transformation* blog (http://jennifershewmaker.com/operation-transformation).

Robyn Silverman
www.drrobynsilverman.com
Child / teen development specialist, body image expert, and author of *Good Girls Don't Get Fat: How Weight Obsession Is Messing Up Our Girls and How We Can Help Them Thrive Despite It*.

Rachel Simmons
www.rachelsimmons.com
Educator and coach who helps girls and young women grow into authentic, emotionally intelligent, and assertive adults and author of *Odd Girl Out: The Hidden Culture of Aggression in Girls* and *The Curse of the Good Girl: Raising Authentic Girls with Courage and Confidence.*

Jess Weiner
www.jessweiner.com
Weiner uses storytelling for social change, specializing in helping brands cultivate positive media and marketing messages targeted toward women and girls. She is the owner of Talk to Jess, LLC, Dove's global ambassador for self-esteem, and author of *A Very Hungry Girl: How I Filled Up on Life . . . and How You Can Too!* and *Life Doesn't Begin 5 Pounds from Now.*

Rosalind Wiseman
http://rosalindwiseman.com
Expert on children, teens, parenting, bullying, social justice, and ethical leadership; author of *Queen Bees and Wannabes: Helping Your Daughter Survive Cliques, Gossip, Boyfriends, and the New Realities of Girl World* and *Masterminds and Wingmen.*

Girl-Positive Organizations

The Achilles Effect (with Crystal Smith)
www.achilleseffect.com

Adios Barbie
www.adiosbarbie.com

Beauty Redefined
www.beautyredefined.net

Brave Girls Want
www.bravegirlswant.com

Campaign for a Commercial-Free Childhood (with Susan Linn)
www.commercialfreechildhood.org

Center on Media and Child Health
www.cmch.tv

Common Sense Media
www.commonsensemedia.org

Feminist Fatale
http://feministfatale.com

Feminist Frequency
www.feministfrequency.com

Fit vs. Fiction (with Marci Warhaft-Nadler)
www.fitvsfiction.com

Geena Davis Institute for Gender in Media
www.seejane.org

Girl Scouts of America
www.girlscouts.org

Girls for a Change
www.girlsforachange.org

Girls Inc.
www.girlsinc.com

Girls on the Run
www.girlsontherun.org

Hardy Girls Healthy Women (with Lyn Mikel Brown)
www.hghw.org

The Illusionists
www.theillusionists.org

The Mamafesto
www.themamafesto.com

A Mighty Girl
www.amightygirl.com

Miss Representation
http://missrep.org

Ms. magazine
www.msmagazine.com/blog

New Moon Girls
www.newmoon.com

Operation Beautiful
www.operationbeautiful.com

Powered by Girl
www.poweredbygirl.org

Princess Free Zone (with Michele Yulo)
www.princessfreezone.com

Reel Girl (with Margot Magowan)
http://reelgirl.com

Sanford Harmony Program
www.sanfordharmonyprogram.org

Shaping Youth
www.shapingyouth.org

SheHeroes
http://sheheroes.org

SPARK Movement
http://sparkmovement.org

Tornado Warning (with Elin Stebbins Waldal)
www.elinstebbinswaldal.com

Women's Media Center
www.womensmediacenter.com

Where to Shop

CP Toys
www.cptoys.com

Eko Bear (Canada)
www.ekobear.ca

Fat Brain Toys
www.fatbraintoys.com

For Small Hands
www.forsmallhands.com

Go! Go! Sports Girls
www.gogosportsgirls.com

Goldie Blox
www.goldieblox.com

Growing Tree Toys
www.growingtreetoys.com

K'nex
www.knex.com

Lalaloopsy
www.lalaloopsy.com

Magic Cabin Toys
www.magiccabin.com

A Mighty Girl
www.amightygirl.com

Pigtail Pals & Ballcap Buddies
www.pigtailpals.com

Polkadot Patch Boutique
www.polkadotpatch.com

Princess Free Zone
www.princessfreezone.com

Rokenbok
www.rokenbok.com

Roominate
www.roominatetoy.com

Sophie & Lili
www.sophieandlili.com

Toward the Stars
www.towardthestars.com

Bibliography

Books

Eliot, Lise. *Pink Brain, Blue Brain: How Small Differences Grow into Troublesome Gaps—and What We Can Do About It*. Boston: Houghton Mifflin Harcourt, 2009.

Farr, Kathryn. *Sex Trafficking: The Global Market in Women and Children*. New York: Worth Publishers, 2005.

Goldman, Carrie. *Bullied: What Every Parent, Teacher, and Kid Needs to Know About Ending the Cycle of Fear*. New York: HarperOne, 2012.

Hartstein, Jennifer L. *Princess Recovery: A How-To Guide to Raising Strong, Empowered Girls Who Can Create Their Own Happily Ever Afters*. Avon, MA: Adams Media, 2012.

Kane, Emily W. *The Gender Trap: Parents and the Pitfalls of Raising Boys and Girls*. New York: New York University, 2012.

Lamb, Sharon, and Lyn Mikel Brown. *Packaging Girlhood: Rescuing Our Daughters from Marketers' Schemes*. New York: St. Martin's Press, 2006.

Levin, Diane E., and Jean Kilbourne. *So Sexy So Soon: The New Sexualized Childhood, and What Parents Can Do to Protect Their Kids*. New York: Ballantine Books, 2008.

Linn, Susan. *The Case for Make Believe: Saving Play in a Commercialized World*. New York: New Press, 2008.

Linn, Susan. *Consuming Kids: The Hostile Takeover of Childhood*. New York: New Press, 2004.

Orenstein, Peggy. *Cinderella Ate My Daughter: Dispatches from the Front Lines of the New Girlie-Girl Culture*. New York: HarperCollins, 2011.

Philyaw, Deesha. *Co-Parenting 101: Helping Your Children Thrive in Two Households After Divorce*. Oakland, CA: New Harbinger Publications, 2013.

Pipher, Mary Bray. *Reviving Ophelia: Saving the Selves of Adolescent Girls*. New York: Putnam, 1994.

Silverman, Robyn J. A., and Dina Santorelli. *Good Girls Don't Get Fat: How Weight Obsession Is Screwing Up Our Girls and What We Can Do to Help Them Thrive Despite It*. Don Mills, Ontario: Harlequin, 2010.

Simmons, Rachel. *The Curse of the Good Girl: Raising Authentic Girls with Courage and Confidence*. New York: Penguin Press, 2009.

Smith, Crystal. *Achilles Effect: What Pop Culture Is Teaching Young Boys About Masculinity*. Bloomington, IN: iUniverse, 2011.

Stone, Tanya Lee. *The Good, the Bad, and the Barbie: A Doll's History and Her Impact on Us*. New York: Viking, 2010.

Warhaft-Nadler, Marci. *The Body Image Survival Guide for Parents: Helping Toddlers, Tweens, and Teens Thrive*. Lemont, PA: Eifrig Pub, 2013.

Wolf, Naomi. *The Beauty Myth: How Images of Beauty Are Used Against Women*. New York: Morrow, 1991.

Web Articles and Reports

AdelaideNow. "Body Image Obsession Starts in Kindy." http://www.adelaidenow.com.au/news/south-australia/body-image-obsession-starts-in-kindy/story-e6frea83-1111117490357.

American Psychological Association (APA). "Report of the APA Task Force on the Sexualization of Girls." http://www.apa.org/pi/women/programs/girls/report.aspx.

Bloom, Lisa. "How to Talk to Little Girls." *Huffington Post*. http://www.huffingtonpost.com/lisa-bloom/how-to-talk-to-little-gir_b_882510.html.

Carroll, Joseph. "Do Americans Want to Be Surprised by the Sex of Their Baby?" Gallup.com. http://www.gallup.com/poll/28180/americans-want-surprised-sex-their-baby.aspx.

Child Development Institute—Parent Guide to Developmental Stages. "Play Is the Work of the Child." http://childdevelopmentinfo.com/child-development/play-work-of-children.shtml.

"Girls and Body Image: Loving the Skin She's In." Education.com. http://www.education.com/magazine/article/Girls_and_Body_Image_Help_Your/.

Ettus, Samantha. "A Brand's Second Mistake: Where Does Lost Chapstick Go from Here?" *Forbes*. http://www.forbes.com/sites/samanthaettus/2011/10/27/chapstick.

Girl Scouts. "Facts and Findings: Physical and Mental Health." http://www.girlscouts.org/research/facts_findings/physical_and_mental_health.asp.

Goodin, Samantha, Alyssa Denberg, Sarah Murnen, and Linda Smolak. "'Putting on' Sexiness: A Content Analysis of the Presence of Sexualizing Characteristics in Girls Clothing." *Sex Roles* 65, no. 1–2 (2011): 1–12. http://link.springer.com/article/10.1007%2Fs11199-011-9966-8.

Manaster, Hillary. "Saw It, but Didn't See It." Superhero Princess. http://superheroprincess.com/2012/09/25/saw-it-but-didnt-see-it.

"Mattel Management Discusses Q2 2012 Results—Earnings Call Transcript—Seeking Alpha." http://seekingalpha.com/article/726681-mattel-management-discusses-q2-2012-results-earnings-call-transcript.

Murnen, Sarah. "Murnen on Sexualized Girls' Clothing." Kenyon College News Room. www.kenyon.edu/x57477.xml.

Murphy, Caryn E. *New Girl Order: Youth, Gender, and Generation in Contemporary Teen Girls' Media* (dissertation, 2011). http://books.google.com/books?id=r0622hFVoIEC&printsec=frontcover#v=onepage&q&f=false.

Richards, Bailey Shoemaker. "The Meeting: When SPARK Met LEGO." SPARK Movement. http://www.sparksummit.com/2012/04/23/the-meeting-when-spark-met-lego.

Sanford Harmony Program. "Conceptual Model." http://sanford.clas.asu.edu/program/research.

Spiers, Melissa. "Chapstick Sticks It to Women." Reel Girl. http://reelgirl.com/2011/10/chapstick-sticks-it-to-women-by-melissa-spiers-guest-post.

"Tap into the Lucrative Tween Market." Business on Main. http://businessonmain.msn.com/browseresources/articles/selling.aspx?cp-documentid=26113914#fbid=F1LLQi5ddn9.

"Teen Health and the Media." University of Washington. http://depts.washington.edu/thmedia/view.cgi?section=bodyimage&page=fastfacts.

Television/DVD

Killing Us Softly 4. DVD. Directed by Jean Kilbourne. Northampton, MA: Media Education Foundation, 2010.

Miss Representation. DVD. Directed by Jennifer Siebel Newsom. New York: Virgil Films, 2012.

Our America: 3 AM Girls. Directed by Darcy Dennett. Los Angeles: OWN Network, 2011, 2012.

Index

achievements, recognition for, 42–44, 58

Achilles Effect, The (Smith), 170–171

activism
    examples of, 179–181, 184–185, 189–191
    kid involvement and, 192, 193–194, 200
    suggestions for, 178–179, 185–189
    Weiner on, 182–184

adopted children, 100, 205

age gaps, in blended families, 52–53

Alter, Leslie Goldman, 144

Amelia to Zora (Chin-Lee), 205

American Academy of Pediatrics, 196

American Psychological Association (APA), 8

Angelou, Maya, 173

appearance, shifting focus from, 42–43, 58

Arreola, Veronica, 22, 23–24

art supplies/projects, 31, 67, 69, 70, 72

authenticity, 169

baby products, 17–19

Barbie
    absence of, 21
    career dolls, 76
    clothing for, 75
    conversations about, 79–80
    critical thinking and, 77, 99
    as gift, 37, 43, 44–45, 120
    playdates and, 50, 65
    at school, 147

"Beauty Comes from the Family Tree" Collage, 205

bikes, 174–176

birthdays. *See* gifts; parties

blended families, 51–55

Bloom, Lisa, 43–44
body image
  actions regarding, 92–95
  babies and, 95–96, 197
  cultural expectations and,
    89–91
  diets and, 30
  grade school and, 99–102
  health care providers and,
    143–146
  media and, 90
  middle and high school and,
    102–104
  preschool years and, 97–99
  promoting positive, 55–56,
    110–111
  sexual agency and, 104–106
  sports and, 67
  talking about, 106–109
  toddler years and, 96–97
  toys and, 27–28
Body Image Survival Guide for Par-
  ents, The (Warhaft-Nadler),
  145–146
Body Language (Russell), 107
body parts, discussing, 26–27
Bogusky, Alex, 162
Boyle, Caitlin, 201
Bratz, 56, 75, 81–83, 147
Bratzillaz, 81–83
Brave Girls Alliance, 185
Britney Effect, 162, 164
Brown, Lyn Mikel, 6, 75, 131–133
Bullied (Goldman), 152
bullying, 149, 152–154. *See also*
  teasing

Campaign for a Commercial-Free
  Childhood, 85, 164
Candie's, 176–178
Care 2, 178, 186
Case for Make Believe, The (Lin), 60
categorization, 61
celebrities, 8, 53, 154, 162, 164
change.org, 178, 179, 180, 185,
  186
Chapman, Brenda, 73
ChapStick, 180, 184
Chin-Lee, Cynthia, 205
choice, importance of, 62
Cinderella Ate My Daughter (Orenstein), 74–75
clothing
  body image and, 93
  cross-gender relationships and,
    170–171
  dress-up, 31, 65
  gendered, 13
  grade school and, 102
  guiding choices of, 104
  for holidays, 113–114
  individuality and, 31, 98, 150
  preschool years and, 98
  sexualization of, 14, 161–162,
    163, 176–178
color
  of baby products, 4, 6, 18–19
  toys and, 64
  variety of, 31
communication
  about clothing, 166–167
  about teasing, 151
  with chain stores, 187–191

with children, 30
conflict and, 55–57
with corporations, 178–179
encouraging, 32
gifts and, 119–121
with health care providers,
    139–140, 141–142
individuality and, 45–46
social media and, 185–187
telling your child's story, 42–43
Consumer Products Safety
    Improvement Act (CPSIA),
    207
Co-Parenting 101 (Philyaw), 52
coparents, 51–55
creativity, encouraging, 31–32, 72,
    77
critical thinking
    media literacy and, 195–196
    at school, 148
    teaching, 99, 132–133, 140–141,
        165
    toys and, 76, 77, 78–83
criticism, responses to, 38, 39–40

dating, 105
Day, Lori, 155, 156
dieting, 108
Disney, 13, 14, 184–185. *See also*
    princess culture (pink culture)
doctors. *See* health care providers
dress codes, 147, 149

eating disorders, 90, 91, 101, 144–
    145. *See also* body image
Edell, Dana, 192–194

educators/schools, 135–137, 145–
    152, 154–158, 159
Einstein, Albert, 172
Eliot, Lise, 62–63
"Empowering Word" Typography
    Collage, 205–206
empowerment, 160
Etsy, 209
expectations
    changing, 41–42
    rigidity of, 87

Facebook, 185–187
family rules, 47
fashion dolls, 75–77
fat talk, 91, 92, 104. *See also* body
    image
food
    body image and, 93
    family meals and, 94
    growing, 102
    healthy, 67
    healthy attitudes toward, 96–97
    meal preparation and, 99
    shopping for, 102
    teaching about, 107–109
Ford, Henry, 136
Fosberry, Jennifer, 205
Foster, Stacie, 61–62, 148
friends, 47–51

gender, play and, 63–64, 155
gender identity, 87
gender neutrality
    in baby announcements, 20
    encouraging, 41, 63–64

gender neutrality (*continued*)
    lack of, 4–5
    in nurseries, 18
    registries and, 19
    requesting, 159–160
    in schools, 157–158
    toys and, 63–64
gender of baby
    finding out in advance, 20
    revealing, 23
gender roles, lack of, 30
gifts, 114–121
Girls for a Change, 181
Girls on the Run, 210–211
glamour girl parties, 121–123
Go! Go! Sports Girls Dolls,
    210–211
Goldman, Carrie, 152–154
Good Girls Don't Get Fat (Silverman), 106

Halloween, 125–131
Hardy Girls Healthy Women, 180
Harkin, Tom, 171
Hartstein, Jennifer, 74, 159–160
health care providers, 135–142,
    143–146, 159
Help, The, 169
holidays, 113–114
homophobia, 153
Huffy, 174–176

"I Am . . ." Silhouette, 202
"I Am Full of Awesome" Digital
    Photo Book, 206
ignorance, willful, 38–39

Indiegogo, 209
infants, products for, 17–18
Internet, 83–84

JCPenney, 179–180, 184
Jussel, Amy, 171–172

KGOY (kids getting older
    younger), 162, 176
Kickstarter, 209
Kilbourne, Jean, 164
Klein, Melanie, 86–87
Kohl's, 176–178

La Dee Da dolls, 81–83
Lamb, Sharon, 6, 75, 163
Leg Avenue, 127
LEGO/LEGO Friends, 180, 184,
    185
Levin, Diane E., 164
Linn, Susan, 60, 71–73, 164

Magowan, Margot, 180, 201–202
Manaster, Hillary, 148, 189–191
marketers, methods of, 131–132,
    162–163
Martinez, Elizabeth, 22
Martinez, Tony, Jr., 22, 23–24
Mattel, 83, 180–181
McDonald's, 142–143
media
    kids shaping their own, 197–201
    parents making their own,
        206–207
media consumption
    in blended families, 52–53

control of, 30
guidelines for, 66, 67
shared, 103
media literacy
body image and, 106–107
lack of attention to, 17
teaching, 99, 132–133, 158,
195–196
tips for, 30–32
Merida, 73, 184–185
MGA, 83
Mighty Girl, A, 204
misogyny, 153
Monster High, 75, 80–81, 83, 147,
180–181
Montessori, Maria, 61
music industry, 163
"My Dreams" Vision Board, 204
My Name Is Not Isabella (Fosberry),
205

nicknames, 21–22
Nordstrom, 189–191
Norgaard, Jodi, 210–211
Novi Stars, 75
nurseries, gender neutrality in, 18
nurses. *See* health care providers
nutrition, 67, 93, 99, 107–109. *See
also* food

Operation Beautiful (Boyle), 201
Operation Transformation, 180
Orenstein, Peggy, 74–75, 180
Oriental Trading Company, 141
"Our Founding Mothers" Reading
and Art Project, 204–205

Packaging Girlhood (Brown and
Lamb), 6, 75
parties
birthday, 114–119
glamour girl, 121–123
as project idea, 204
suggestions for, 124–125
personal brands, 81, 84, 93,
167–171
Philyaw, Deesha, 52
Pigtail Pals & Ballcap Buddies,
15, 49, 141, 179–180, 207
Pink Brain, Blue Brain (Eliot),
62–63
Pipher, Mary, 105
plasticity, 63
play
coed, 63–64
cross-gender, 155
pretend, 60
role of, 60–61
playdates, 47–48, 50–51, 65
Postman, Neil, 71
Powered by Girl, 180
pretend play, 60
Princess, as nickname, 21–22
princess culture (pink culture), 21,
73–75
Princess Free Zone, 180, 208–209
Princess Recovery (Hartstein), 74
project ideas, 202–206
puberty, 102

redefining girly, meaning of, 14–16
Reel Girl, 180
registries, baby, 17, 19

restaurants, 142–143
Reviving Ophelia (Pipher), 105
Russell, Susan, 107

Sanford Harmony Program
 (SHP), 61, 63, 148, 155
school, 146–152, 154–158
Sea World, 192
self-esteem, 107. *See also* body
 image
self-image, positive, 92. *See also*
 body image
self-objectification, 8, 105
service parties, 125
sex trade, 127–128
sexual agency, 104–106
sexuality
 body image and, 104–106
 discussing, 26–27
sexualization
 bikes and, 174–176
 bullying and, 153
 effects of, 8–9
 internalization of, 8
 vs. sexuality, 8
 See also clothing; toys
Shewmaker, Jennifer W., 33–34,
 180
shopping, guidelines for, 164–165
Silverman, Robyn, 106, 110–111
Simmons, Rachel, 28–29
slut-shaming, 36
SmileMakers, 141
Smith, Crystal, 170–171
Smith, Whitney, 181

So Sexy So Soon (Levin and Kilbourne), 164
social media, 83–85, 179–180,
 184–185, 207
Society 6, 209
SPARK Movement, 180, 192
Spears, Britney, 162, 164
Spiers, Melissa, 180
sports, 67–68, 98–99, 101
stepparents/stepchildren,
 51–55
stereotypes
 bullying and, 152–154
 challenging, 26, 41, 47–48,
  61–62, 63
 critical thinking and, 148
 marketing and, 9
 reinforcement of, 62
 toys and, 61
storytelling, 198–200
support, lack of, 36–38, 172

Task Force on the Sexualization of
 Girls, 8
teachers. *See* educators/schools
teasing, 100–101, 149, 150,
 151–154
technology, 83–85
television, 31, 55–56, 60, 65, 72,
 133, 196
Theme Song Party, 204
Time Capsule Message, 203
toys
 body image and, 27–28
 changes in, 44–45

color and, 64
critical thinking and, 76, 77,
    78–83
gender neutrality and, 63–64
gender stereotypes and, 61
gendered, 4–5, 60
guidelines for, 64–71
influencer meetings on, 180–181
role of, 59, 60
sexualization and, 49–50, 56–57,
    75–77
technology and, 83–85
Twitter, 185–187

vlogging, 186–187
volunteer opportunities, 68, 101

Warhaft-Nadler, Marci, 145–146
Weiner, Jess, 181, 182–184
Winx Club, 81–83
Wiseman, Rosalind, 57–58

"Year of Empowerment, A" Calen-
    dar and Mixed Media, 206
"You Are Special Because . . ."
    Mobile, 203
Yulo, Michele, 208–209

About the Author

Melissa Atkins Wardy is the founder of Pigtail Pals & Ballcap Buddies, a company that sells empowering and inspirational children's apparel and products, and runs a blog of the same name focused on gender stereotypes and sexualization in childhood. Wardy discusses these issues facing families with thousands of parents using social media and workshops. She is also the cofounder of The Brave Girls Alliance, a gender equality think tank and advocacy group dedicated to communicating with and influencing media, corporations, and retailers.

She has appeared on CNN and FOX News and in the *Boston Globe*, *New York Daily News*, *Huffington Post*, and the *Ms. Magazine* blog, which have featured her work and her campaigns against national brands and retailers that resulted in the removal of sexist ads and products. She lives in Janesville, Wisconsin, with her husband and two children.